Entrepreneurship is a Mind-Set not a Storefront

Yolanda Conley Shields

Copyright © 2016 Yolanda Conley Shields

All rights reserved.

ISBN-10:151914654X
ISBN-13: 9781519146540

INTRODUCTION

Entrepreneurship is a Mindset not a Storefront

I always tell people that entrepreneurship is in my blood. I remember growing and watching and listening my grandfather Robert Brooks talk about his businesses. I loved seating next to him when he would visit Nashville, TN from Anchorage Alaska. My Grandfather would come to visit us in the Spring or Fall. He never liked coming in the summer. He lived in Alaska and always thought it was too hot in the summer and too cold in the winter. In 1950 people generally recognized that the nation's economy, and financial performance of its businesses would affect every American personally. My grandfather understood that the security of his business, how much he earned doing it, the cost of the goods and services, the price he paid to borrow money, and the interest he received by saving was all directly related to the health of the economy.

As an African American it meant even more because if he did well others would get the opportunity to start a business because they saw someone that looked like them do it and succeed. During the 1950s the American economy was the strongest in the world which really was a benefit for my grandfather.

I knew as a young girl that I would have my own business but didn't know what it would be. I remember writing in my diary and journals the many things I wanted to do. I still have those journals and read them at least once a year to remind myself of the goals I had and what I have been able to accomplish. In every journal I listed a business I would start. Now when I read them I laugh because some of the names were very funny. Some of them I started and some I helped others to start. I believe that God has great plans for all of us and he sometimes does it in different ways. As I run my business today the many lessons from my grandfather ring in my ear a lot. My grandfather inspired me to reach for the stars because there were no limits. Watching him and hearing the many stories about how he ran his businesses let me know that I could do anything I put my mind to.

If he could run a successful business in the 50's and 60's as an African American man I knew I could do it. The main things I took away from him is 1. Work hard 2. Don't allow people to put limits on you. 3. Learn your business 4. Surround yourself with people that encourage and support you. My mom would share with me that he was a very smart business man that understood that it took multiple streams of income. He started several business in the area of construction, equipment and car rental and property management. People in his city respected him and knew he was a man that believed in hard work, integrity and was determined to achieve his business goals. So I knew as a young child what it took to have a mind of an entrepreneur because my grandfather modeled it. Even with the struggles during the 1950's racial tensions he still did well.

Entrepreneurship is a vital movement in all areas of our society, empowering individuals to seek opportunities where others see defeat or crises. For many years, entrepreneurs have created many great businesses that led to job creation, improved productivity, increased prosperity, and a higher quality of life. Entrepreneurship is now playing a vital role in finding solutions to the huge problems facing our communities, in the area of health, education, technology and environment. It takes an entreprenerers mind to make this happen. Many books have been written to help educate others about entrepreneurship. This book will focus on the mindset and sustainability of entrepreneurship.

The entrepreneurship movement around the world over the past 50 years has had an impact globally. While there is opportunities for improvement and innovation, many entreprenerers have started a ripple effect around the globe. Technology and social media has played a major role in growing businesses globally. Some people think entrepreneurship is just about setting up an office, but It is more than that. It is a mindset that drives a person to want to run his or her own business. It is definitely hard work to start and sustain your own business. You will want to quite the first week if your mindset is not on point.

The purpose of this book is to examine what "mindset" makes an entrepreneur, and what of that mindset will truly make an entrepreneur successful and able to sustain their business. Whenever you see someone that is much more successful and living the life that you have always dreamed off, what is the first thing that comes into a persons mind? "How do they do it"? "Entrepreneurship is a Mindset not a Store Front" will show you how to: create a mindset that shapes your understanding of how to stay focused and what it takes to keep you moving and being innovative in order to accomplish what would be worthwhile; create great ideas, seize new opportunities, create change that makes breakthroughs; build transformational long term sustainable business and a dynamic vibrant entrepreneurial atmosphere within your business.

"Entrepreneurship is a Mindset not a Store Front" is about what it will take to keep your mind focused so that you succeed in an unpredictable world. It will help everyone from seasoned business leaders, young entrepreneurs and corporate leaders of large corporations to come up with innovative business ideas that others miss and act on them to build the truly entrepreneurial organizations of the future.

The human mind has been developed in such a way that we tend to think about things that we don't want in life rather than thinking about things that we do want. Research has proven that the law of attraction is powerful. What we think in our mind is what we do. This book will show what the right mindset will do when we focus on the following things Essential Characteristics Of The Entrepreneurial Mind, Common Characteristics of Successful Entrepreneurs, Effective Networking, Social Entrepreneurship, Principles of Business Integrity, Negotiations and Business Pitch, Innovative Visionary Entrepreneurs, Leadership Principles and Social Entrepreneurship.

CONTENTS

Introduction

Acknowledgments

1	4 Essential Characteristics Of Entrepreneurial Mind	1
2	Idea Evaluation Checklist	17
3	Entrepreneur SHIFT Building Blocks to Success	19
4	Benefits of networking for Entrepreneurs	50
5	Common Characteristics of Successful Entrepreneurs	55
6	Successful Entrepreneurs	59
7	Social Entrepreneurship	66
8	Leadership Principles for Entrepreneurs	72
9	Negotiations and Business Pitch	79
10	Entrepreneur Resources and Quotes	87

ACKNOWLEDGMENTS

There are a great many people I want to thank for their extra efforts in helping me to get to this place in my career and entrepreneur journey. First and foremost, I would like to thank my family, friends and the many mentors throughout this journey that have encouraged me along the way to complete this book. Many of these people pushed me encouraged me, also opened doors for me.

My late grandfather Robert Brooks was definitely one of the people that has inspired me over the years. He taught me by modeling what it takes to persevere as a business owner. My sister Iris Nance started her business years ago and I have watched her build a successful business while being a mother and wife. To my mother who always encouraged me and believed I could do anything I put my mind to. The many teachers and coaches from high school and college that taught me that hard work pays off. Big thank you to all those that shared their entrepreneur journey in the book. I know what they have shared will encourage many of you to finish strong.

Chapter 1
4 Essential Characteristics Of Entrepreneurial Mindset

Strategic

Unshakable

Risk Taker

Ethical

STRATEGIC: Being strategic is key to sustaining yourself as an entrepreneur. You can wish all day to have your own business, but if you are not strategic in your approach it will not happen nor will it last. Most people think they are strategic because they have completed a strategic plan. There are misguided, but popular views that say that strategic thinking is for long term planning (but it is needed immediately and long term).

I believe that "strategic thinkers" intentionally use their assets (like skill or special resources) to take advantage of all opportunities that may be on the table or haven't even arrived yet. "Strategic thinking" is the thought that is put into using assets, neutralizing vulnerabilities, taking advantage of opportunity, and positioning oneself to succeed.

Strategic Thinking

Strategic Thinking is a planning process that applies innovation, strategic planning and operational planning to develop business strategies that have a greater chance for success.

More and more organizations are learning that past experience is not always the best basis for developing future strategies. Executives need to thoughtfully consider how to create value for their clients. The exercise of strategic planning, while important, tends to answer the "how" and "when" of business planning and rarely captures the essence of what it means to think strategically. That's where strategic thinking comes in. Strategic thinking is the **"what:"** and **"why"** of the planning process. It answers the question, "What should we be doing, and why?"

Strategic Thinking requires innovation and creativity and includes a research phase to examine the voice of the customer, the employee and industry best practices. It is a process of examining everything we do in our various roles, understanding the needs of our customers and ensuring that all of this is linked to clearly defined strategic imperatives.

If we compare strategic thinking with strategic planning and operational planning we see that:

- *Strategic Thinking* – is the "What" and the "Why"…that is what should we be doing and why.

- *Strategic Planning* – is the "How" and "When" …at a very high level.
- *Operational Planning* – is the specific details of the how and when.

Strategic Growth

Businesses are under constant pressure to grow. Growth means higher profitability and greater returns for the owners. It also means the company is succeeding in the competitive struggle. Strategic thinking forces companies to recognize they cannot afford to stand still. They must be innovative in all aspects of the operation of the business. A company cannot continue to do things the same way year after year because they will end up losing market share to companies that are not afraid of change.

Improved Decision Making

Business owners that make strategic thinking a central element of their management philosophy often become better strategic thinkers as time goes on. They learn how to recognize subtle changes in the business environment that will have a direct impact on their revenues--things they may have missed before. They become more adept at predicting how competitors are likely to react to the strategies they implement. They begin to view the business as their customers see it, and formulate strategies so they do a more capable job of reaching new potential customers. Strategic thinking enables a business owner to make more logical, confident decisions.

Moses

We see clearly in Scripture that Moses was a strategic thinker—or at least he learned to be. Moses was struggling as a leader soon after he led the nation of Israel out of Egypt. His father-in-law, Jethro, came to see him after hearing the incredible things God had been doing. Jethro observed that Moses was overwhelmed with the burdens of leadership and shared with him a God-given plan—a strategy—for dealing with the issue.

When the National Cancer Institute chose to focus its research efforts on neutralizing the enzyme that spreads cancer rather than on curing cancer, it was shifting its strategic target in order to combat this dreadful disease.

Nehemiah

Nehemiah was a God-appointed leader who used a strategy. When God laid it on his heart to rebuild the walls of Jerusalem, Nehemiah began to establish and then work through a well-planned strategy to accomplish the vision God had given. He assessed the damage. He secured the resources. He established leaders and distributed the assignments among them.

When a software development firm chooses to buck the tide and not offer products and services for the Microsoft environment but provide an alternative to MS in the market place, it is making a courageous (we don't know if it will be successful) strategic decision

"However beautiful the strategy, you should occasionally look at the results." (Winston Churchill)

The Key to being a Strategic Thinker:

The way you become a strategic thinker is being around and working with those that are. You BECOME WHO YOU ARE AROUND! It also relates to how you make decisions your business idea or your career. Those that are strategic thinkers use this approach when thinking about personal skills in order to take advantage of opportunities that come their way.

The focus for strategic questions is similar for each individual and for a business, even though the individual has a smaller scope and less complexity. In order to grow in this area facilitation it takes strategic thought at the level of one-on-one coaching, and small group meetings.

When you are STRATEGIC THINKER you:

- Reframe problems to get to the bottom of things, in terms of root causes
- Challenge current beliefs and mindsets, including your own
- Uncover hypocrisy, manipulation, and bias in organizational decisions

"The essence of strategy is choosing what not to do." (*Michael Porter*)

"Strategic Thinking is a leadership tool which will help a Business owner do a better job focusing the Energy of its staff, and ensuring that they are all working toward the same goals."

UN·SHAK·A·BLE -A belief, feeling, or opinion) strongly felt and unable to be changed:

Many entrepreneurs have strived to become a leader that is unshakable but the economic trails have push the limits on that, but then the hardship will reveal if you are unshakable. No matter what you read or what you are told, you are in control of how you lead your company. Choose not to let negative thoughts dominate your mind. Think about the increased productivity instead of how difficult it will be.

Make the decision to think about success rather than defeat. The more you do it, the easier it becomes. Surrounding yourself with unshakable leaders can be contagious. Spend time with and engage those motivated and successful people you know.

Don't be shaken by ideas that don't make it. Less than 1% of ideas last more than a few years, so don't take a single failure as a sign that you aren't a capable entrepreneur. Numbers don't mean much to an entrepreneur. It's about your unshakeable will and your unusual vision.
BE ORIGINAL-BE INNOVATIVE

You have to out-work and out-think everyone else. You have to predict where your market is going based on several factors that others may not be seeing. You are the new truth. BELIEVE IT AND RECIEVE IT, and your chances of succeeding are 50/50!"

RISK TAKER – is someone who risks loss or injury in the hope of gain or excitement.

Risk is the potential of loss (an undesirable outcome, however not necessarily so) resulting from a given action, activity and/or inaction. The notion implies that a choice having an influence on the outcome sometimes exists (or existed). Potential losses themselves may also be called "risks". Any human endeavor carries some risk, but some are much riskier than others. You might not actually be climbing Mount Everest, but sometimes the important things we're called to do can feel the same.

Twenty years from now you will be more disappointed by the things you didn't do than by the ones you did. So throw off the bowlines, sail away from the safe harbor, catch the trade winds in your sails. Explore. Dream. Discover." -- Mark Twain.

So many times we avoid those difficult moments that put us out of our comfort zone. We might not flat out deny these opportunities, but we delay and let them pass. Here are some things to remember when it comes to taking risks. Risk implies the chance that things might not work out. Risk makes us feel powerful and without some Risk we and just not going to **GROW**

What is the worst that could happen? When we take risk we should think about the outcomes positive and negative. Risk also includes WISDOM! It's ok to seek out wise counsel. I wouldn't seek out advise from someone that has never taken a RISK.

Risk stretches us and takes us out of our comfort zone and helps us grow. It is getting out of our comfort zone and doing something different is when we learn something new about ourselves.

Don't let fear stop you. FEAR = False Evidence Appearing Real – This can be our biggest obstacle if we let it. The biggest fear we usually have is will I be a failure. It all depends on who definition you are working with. As I research many inventors I realize that many of their ideas would not have come to pass if they took no Risk. Many inventions wouldn't have been realized without the **RISK TAKERS!** I use to be told that I should always be safe and not take Risk! If I had listened I wouldn't be where I am today. I am Stronger and wiser because of the decisions I made that may have appeared foolish or crazy.

What if your opportunities or dreams were delayed because you didn't take a risk? I think that is the case for many of us. I don't want to be seating 10 or 15 years down the road and wondering what could have been if I would have taken some RISK! Great businesses are built on taking a few Risks.

"Security is mostly a superstition. Life is either a daring adventure or nothing." -- Helen Keller

You feel most alive when you're doing what you were made to do. We all should grow and not stay the same. If you look back over your life and you are in the same place you were 10 years ago you are not living your **BEST LIFE**.

RISK-TAKERS: Risk taking is not about being foolhardy. The innovator risk-taker brings good judgment and self-awareness to everything, but understands that there is a point – beyond the safe, beyond the secure – where there are disproportionate rewards. In any organization, there are plenty of fumbles, missteps, train wrecks, and failures. But these are less the result of risk-taking, and more of no planning and experience. Look for the places in your organization where there is lots of homework being done, lots of direct, plain conversation and a strong sense of fun, and you'll find the risk-takers there. Risk-takers resist the temptation of the status quo and continuously push organizations into new – and quite possibly innovative – areas. *Warren Zevon Forbes*

"Yes, risk-taking is inherently failure-prone. Otherwise, it would be called 'sure-thing-taking.'" -- Jim McMahon

Some of the most famous - RISK TAKERS

Mark Pincus, 43

Founder and CEO of Zynga, an online social gaming company (creator of "FarmVille" and "Mafia Wars") Greatest risk? Saying no to my last chance at funding for my (first) company Freeloader in 1996.

Candace Cameron Bure, 33

Actress, played "D.J. Tanner" on *Full House* - My biggest risk was stepping away from the entertainment industry at such a young age. Following *Full House*, I got married at 20 and moved to Canada with my husband to support him. I took 10 years off from the entertainment industry to raise my family: 3 children and a husband of 13 years. (Happy ending: In 2009, Cameron Bure returned to TV as Summer Van Horn on ABC's *Make it or Break It*.)

Tim Westergren, 44

Founder of Pandora Radio In the winter of 2001, Pandora was out of money. We had a choice: cut our losses and throw in the towel or find a way to keep going. We decided to keep the company alive and start deferring salaries. Ultimately, over 50 people deferred almost $1.5 million over the course of two years (a practice that is illegal in California). When we were finally rescued by an investment in 2004, I had maxed-out 11 credit cards.

Vivian Jones, along with James Hood, were the two students escorted through the doors of The University of Alabama by the National Guard after being barred from enrolling in June of 1963. The following day civil rights activist Medgar Evers was shot to death in Jackson, Miss. Instead of hiding in her dorm room or giving up and leaving the university, Vivian went to class that day, and eventually went on to become the first black woman to graduate from The University of Alabama in 1965. During a time when the south was in a fierce civil rights debate, taking this step was not only risky, it was revolutionary.

Trip Jennings has paddled white water to explore rivers around the world and in 2008 made a first descent of the notoriously turbulent lower Congo River.

Patrick Meier was sitting in his Medford, Massachusetts, apartment when the January 2010 earthquake struck Haiti. The 35-year-old Tufts Ph.D. candidate was soon assisting quake victims—without even leaving home. Opening his laptop, he mobilized hundreds of volunteers to scrape data points from tweets, text messages, UN reports, and more to build a constantly updated online map. His efforts guided citizens, aid workers, and the U.S. Coast Guard; experts say the map likely saved hundreds of lives. Meier, a Swiss citizen who grew up in Africa, now maps crises all over the world.

Barrington Irving became the youngest person (and first African American) to fly solo around the world when the 23-year-old landed in Miami on June 27, 2007. The former high school football star had been studying aviation for only a year when he went after sponsors to help him assemble a single-engine plane for the 27,000-mile journey. Irving says he took on the trip to inspire young people to grow stronger by testing the limits of their capabilities. Today he is both a pilot and a teacher, using his experience to encourage kids in Florida to explore the skies.

Sunita Williams assumed as a kid that *The Jetsons* and *Star Trek* signaled a future where space travel would be routine. She never dreamed she'd be one of the pioneers. The former Navy pilot, age 47, has spent 322 days in space and 50 hours walking in space—the most spacewalking of any female astronaut. She first met astronauts two decades ago during test pilot school—and discovered that with her flying experience, she could join them. Now, as a member of the astronaut corps, she draws upon her Navy background. Walking in space, she says, is like flying a helicopter with a battle group: You focus on your job but always know where the other guy is.

ETHICAL

Ethics is a branch of philosophy that addresses questions about morality and it is the very important subject for all people. There are two levels of ethics; theoretical and applied ethics. Business ethics is one of the important branches of the applied ethics. These ethical philosophies have their positive and negative sides.

If recent history teaches us anything is that ethics and character count, especially in business. Huge organizations like J.P. Morgan Securities LLC, Enron, Arthur Andersen, Fannie Mae were damaged by what I think were executives consumed with greed and no moral compass. If you don't have integrity, you have nothing. You can't buy it. You can have all the money in the world, but if you are not a moral and ethical person, you really have nothing.

Definition, of ethical principles are universal standards of right and wrong prescribing the kind of behavior an ethical company or person should and should not engage in. These principles provide a guide to making decisions but they also establish the criteria by which your decisions will be judged by others.

As you lead in your business and life, how people judge your character is critical to long-term success because it is the foundation of trust and credibility. Both can be destroyed by actions which are, unethical. Successful executives must be concerned with both their character and their reputation.

"Those of us who believe in God and derive our sense of right and wrong and ethics from God's Word really have no difficulty whatsoever defining where our ethics come from. People who believe in survival of the fittest might have more difficulty deriving where their ethics come from. A lot of evolutionists are very ethical people".
Benjamin Carson

Abraham Lincoln described character as the tree and reputation as the shadow. Your character is what you really are; your reputation is what people think of you.

7 Ethical Principles:

HONESTY - The quality or condition of being honest; integrity. Truthfulness; sincerity - Act fairly and honestly with those who are affected by our actions and treat them as we would expect them to treat us if the situation were reversed.

INTEGRITY - Steadfast adherence to a strict moral or ethical code. The state of being unimpaired; soundness.

LOYALTY - The state or quality of being loyal. A feeling or attitude of devoted attachment and affection.

CARING - Feeling and exhibiting concern and empathy for others

COMMITMENT TO EXCELLENCE - The state, quality, or condition of excelling; superiority Something in which one excels.

ACCOUNTABLITY - The obligation of an individual or organization to account for its activities, accept responsibility for them, and to disclose the results in a transparent manner. It also includes the responsibility for money or other entrusted property.

TRANSPARENT - a situation in which business and financial activities are done in an open way without secrets, so that people can trust that they are fair and honest:

In the research study, "Does Business Ethics Pay?" by The Institute of Business Ethics (IBE), it was found that companies displaying a "clear commitment to ethical conduct" consistently outperform companies that do not display ethical conduct. The Director of IBE, Philippa

Foster Black, stated: "Not only is ethical behavior in business life the right thing to do in principle, we have shown that it pays off in financial returns." These findings deserve to be considered as an important insight for companies striving for long-term success and growth.

Entrepreneur Mindset Checklist

There is a certain mindset I believe you should poses in order to move forward as an entrepreneur. Which do you have and what do you need to work on?

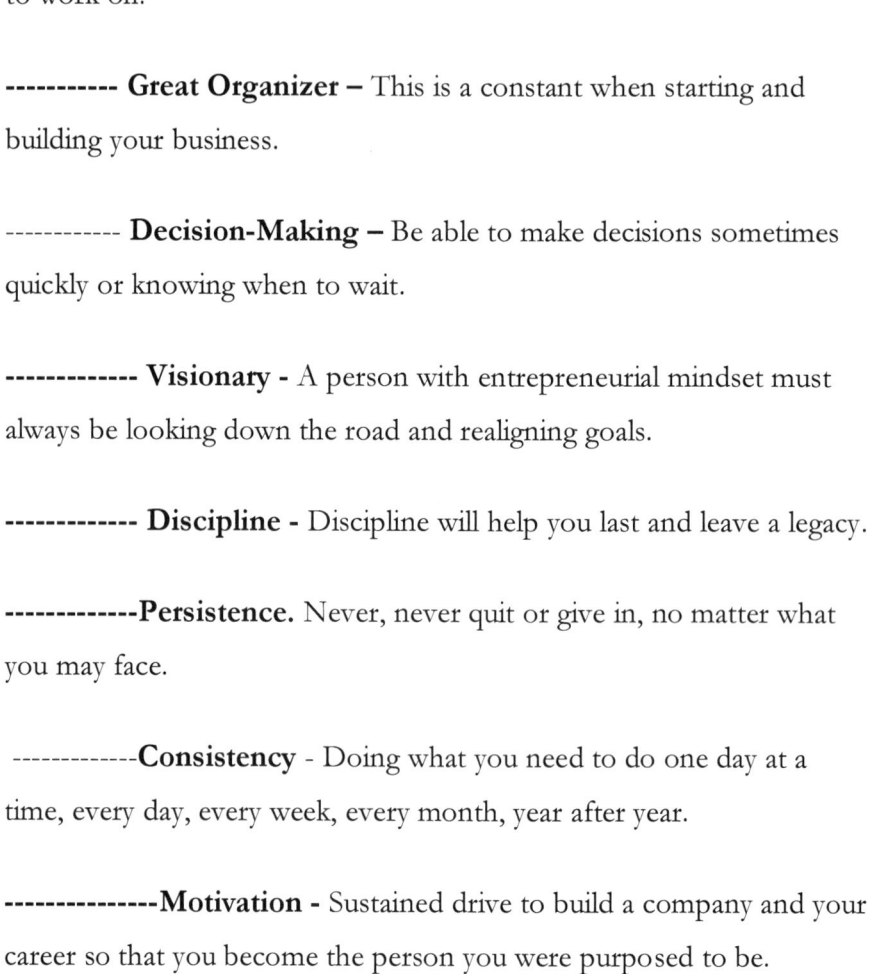

----------- **Great Organizer** – This is a constant when starting and building your business.

------------ **Decision-Making** – Be able to make decisions sometimes quickly or knowing when to wait.

------------- **Visionary** - A person with entrepreneurial mindset must always be looking down the road and realigning goals.

------------- **Discipline** - Discipline will help you last and leave a legacy.

-------------**Persistence.** Never, never quit or give in, no matter what you may face.

-------------**Consistency** - Doing what you need to do one day at a time, every day, every week, every month, year after year.

---------------**Motivation** - Sustained drive to build a company and your career so that you become the person you were purposed to be.

Chapter 2
Idea Evaluation Checklist

Princeton Creative Research has developed an excellent criteria checklist for evaluating ideas that is particularly well-suited to the entrepreneur. Ask yourself the following questions when evaluating an idea for a business or a product

- ○ Have you considered all the advantages or benefits of the idea? Is there a real need for it?
- ○ Have you pinpointed the exact problems or difficulties your idea is expected to solve?
- ○ Is your idea an original, new concept, or is it a new combination or adaptation?
- ○ What immediate or short-range gains or results can be anticipated? Are the projected returns adequate? Are the risk factors acceptable?
- ○ What long-range benefits can be anticipated?
- ○ Have you checked the idea for faults or limitations?
- ○ Are there any problems the idea might create? What are the changes involved?
- ○ How simple or complex will the idea's execution or implementation be?
- ○ Could you work out several variations of the idea? Could you offer alternative ideas?
- ○ Does your idea have a natural sales appeal? Is the market ready for it? Can customers afford it? Will they buy it? Is

there a timing factor?

- o What, if anything, is your competition doing in this area? Can your company be competitive?
- o Have you considered the possibility of user resistance or difficulties?
- o Does your idea fill a real need, or does the need have to be created through promotional and advertising efforts?
- o How soon could the idea be put into operation?

As you can see by the examples mentioned above, there are many methods available with which to evaluate your idea. You should pick and choose the criteria that best suit your needs, depending on the type of company and/or the type of product you seek to evaluate.

Chapter 3
Entrepreneur Shift
Building Blocks to Success

Hannah Paramore ~ President CEO Paramore Digital

Like many entrepreneurs, I became a business owner by accident. I was raised by a family that was in the ministry, my father a preacher and my mother a housewife. The piano was my first love and so when it came time to go to college that is what I pursued. I didn't think about a career because that was not my model.

But things worked out differently for me, and a couple marriages and two children later I was in my mid-thirties providing for my family. I'd worked up through administrative jobs to middle management at various companies, improving as I went along and trying to reconcile with the fact that I didn't get to do what I thought my calling was, which was to focus on my family.

Toward the end of my second marriage, after a layoff gave me 6 month's severance I had the first space of time since my teens when I didn't have to report to work. I was ecstatic for a day, then panicked about the future, amazed at how quickly 3:00 PM came and then frustrated because I felt so unproductive. It was only a few weeks before a recruiter landed me the job that changed my life in the Internet industry.

CitySearch.com was the first start-up I had ever worked with. I loved the pace, the newness, the young staff, and the fact that I learned something every day. It was exciting. The first three years were non-stop. My kids were growing as my marriage was dying and being able to focus on something positive was the thing that got me through the end of that marriage.

Internet companies either matured early or died quickly in those days. I'm not sure which one CitySearch did, but after 3 years the company was at a turning point and it was time for me to move on. This was early 2000 and the first dot com bust was happening. It wasn't hard for me to find a job during that time, but it was hard to keep one. They disappeared over night. For the first time I had a period of instability in my career, going through 4 jobs in 2 years. At each change, however, I learned valuable lessons about how to manage change, how to network to create opportunities and how to unwind a company. And with each I made more and more money.

I also became more and more frustrated. What those companies needed from me more than anything was my contacts. I began to understand that as each new job gave me opportunities to work with someone I'd met in a previous job. Relationships are the most important thing in the world.

During those years when everything was new on the Internet, everybody sold forward. We sold possibility, not actuality. That sounds great until you realize that your client's budgets focus on actuality – they actually need you to do what you say you will do. Maybe this was one of the biggest problems with the Internet in those days. You can stay in business for a little while on the hope that something will pay off, but before too long you have to start delivering. Everything was possible. Little was delivered…

…which is a problem when you are the one who has brought your relationships to the table.

As my 4th job during that time period wound down, I was angry and disappointed in the industry that I had loved. I felt stupid for putting my family's well-being at stake for one crazy job after another. My phone rang off the hook with job offers…from 25-year-olds with the next big idea, and I realized that the most important thing in the world to me is being able to do what I say I will do.

I want this on my tombstone...

She did what she said she would.

I realized that I actually felt safer on my own than working for any of the people who were offering me jobs, and that's when it happened. The Entrepreneurial Flip.

From the moment I decided to take the leap, everything clicked. I had 4 contracts in 2 weeks. After 5 years I looked at our client list and realized that every name on the list could be tied back to someone I met at one of those 4 jobs.

Owning a business in America is a privilege and a blessing. It's also hard. It doesn't always come about the way you think it will, and many of your plans don't work out. But I have learned that if you follow the relationship and are true to your word, things work out better than you could ever have planned.

Iris Conley Nance, Owner of Nance Farmers Insurance Agency

If you had told me 17 years ago that I would own a business, my response would have been "not in a million years". And now fast forward to the present, and I am in that place that I never would have imagined. One of the best employment experiences of my professional career was 10 ½ years as a Bank Examiner with the Federal Deposit Insurance Corporation (FDIC). I saw firsthand what I viewed as financially savvy and successful individuals and Fortune 500 corporations lose everything because of a failed investment or they fell victim to the sour economy. And from that moment, I vowed that I would never go into business for myself.

I remember like it was yesterday saying to my colleagues, "you could not pay me to be a business owner". Now one would have to wonder what in the world changed my mind. I can say that my perspective changed when I married my best friend, Benford, and had my twin daughters, Ashley and Megan. After an 18 month stint with a large financial institution as a Real Estate Finance Credit Analyst, I received a timely recruiting mailer from Farmers Insurance, one of the country's largest insurers of vehicles, homes and small businesses. I was immediately sold on the opportunity to not only have a flexible schedule but also be in control of my income. I also liked the fact that I would be able to help people something I had always enjoyed doing.

I can say that this journey has been one of the hardest with a lot of long hours and some sleepless nights and getting thru the first 5-7 years was a huge challenge. But the ultimate reward was my children looking out from their various cheerleading, orchestra, rowing and other school functions/activities and seeing their parents' proud faces. I also revel in fact that I stand here, 17 years later, with one of the best performing Farmers Insurance affiliated agencies in the state of Virginia and the recipient of various awards and recognition from my district, region and territory. For anyone who is a little hesitant to take that leap of faith to start a new business venture, I would first strongly recommend having available liquid reserves to supplement those periods that cash flow is not as plentiful. I have seen many agents lose the battle because they came into the business already financially deficient. Also, surround yourself with other successful business owners.

I can attest to the fact that the work ethic they exemplify definitely rubs off. Include in your circle individuals who don't mind sharing what has contributed to their success. Stay informed of the latest technology and advances in your field of work. I am constantly reading and have become so excited about learning more about the industry in which I serve. I cannot stress enough the importance of spending the time early on to hire the right people, a principle I learned the hard way. Invest in the best and the brightest who are also team players and management of them becomes easy.

And lastly, be willing to give back to your community whether it is hiring someone who otherwise would not have had the opportunity to getting involved and contributing time and resources to your favorite nonprofit. In summary, love what you do. Hard work and dedication definitely separates the success stories from the casualties. I live by the old Confucius quote that says, "Find something you love to do and you will never have to work for the rest of your life". And proudly I can say that is exactly what I have done. I would like to especially thank my husband and children, Benford, Ashley and Megan. You mean everything to me, and I could not have weathered this journey without your undying support.

Ray Guzman, CEO of WPC Healthcare

Entrepreneurship means many things to me but the easiest, most succinct, definition is not accepting status quo. It is about having the courage, vision, and drive, to create a different outcome. Entrepreneurs are not only those that dare to start their own businesses, but can also be thought leaders and visionaries within existing businesses as well. In fact, in many cases, entrepreneurs have done both – started businesses and also worked within existing ones as well. It's about bringing a perspective, a different perspective, your perspective, to the table. It is about combining expertise and experience to make a difference for others and hopefully for the masses.

Often, people confuse entrepreneurialism with innovation. This confusion further drives the narrative that being an entrepreneur requires a world changing vision, product, or service. And it is that very narrative that discourages many from participating in one of the most powerful and liberating experiences – using your talents to create your preferred future. While it is true that innovative ideas often turn into entrepreneurial businesses, the two are not inextricably linked. Innovation is most often incremental, meaning that an entirely new concept or invention is not a requirement for being entrepreneurial. As an example, starting a restaurant is hardly a new concept, but that doesn't mean that incremental innovations cannot occur. A unique angle or approach to serving customers can be quite innovative and often creates a unique business opportunity in the process.

Sometimes, the very things that frustrate you as a consumer can be an opportunity for your entrepreneurial side to shine. A great example of that is Netflix. Here is a brief explanation of how Netflix came to be, as told by the founder, Reed Hastings:

"I got the idea for Netflix after my company was acquired. I had a big late fee for "Apollo 13." It was six weeks late and I owed the video store $40. I had misplaced the cassette. It was all my fault. I didn't want to tell my wife about it. And I said to myself, "I'm going to compromise the integrity of my marriage over a late fee?" Later, on my way to the gym, I realized they had a much better business model. You could pay $30 or $40 a month and work out as little or as much as you wanted."[1]

As evidenced by the Netflix story, and many others, the entrepreneurial idea of "there has to be a better way" can often lead to an active desire to pursue an idea that may lead you to start your own business. When intuition meets purpose and births a vision, entrepreneurialism is sure to follow.

Lastly, it's important to note that entrepreneurialism can often become a pathway to economic freedom. When it comes to desire, drive, and determination, no one has the "market cornered". The merit and execution of your idea will stand on its own two feet. The market will not predetermine the outcome but rather respond to your entrepreneurship based on how well you meet its needs. If done well, a positive economic outcome will occur and likely increase your willingness to scratch your next entrepreneurial itch given that you'll have achieved some measure of success from following your intuition before.

1 Out of Africa, Onto the Web. As told to AMY ZIPKIN. Published by the New York Times on December 17, 2006.

Linda Fields, President of 7 M~Pact and Executive Director of Joseph and Company

The Spirit of an Entrepreneur ~ Got a problem? Create a solution.

When I consider what it means to be an entrepreneur, I am intrigued to explore the core meaning of entrepreneurship by asking questions such as these:

What is the driving force behind an entrepreneur's zeal to innovate? What habits, thought patterns, or desires are found in the entrepreneurial mindset? What results are derived from entrepreneurial activity?

The term entrepreneur normally refers to bringing new products or services to market assuming a financial risk. I find this definition lacking or insufficient when I ponder the spirit that resides in the heart and mind of an entrepreneur. Probing further, I landed on an expanded definition of the word, which begins to touch the spirit of an entrepreneur.

According to Dictionary.com, Entrepreneurs, in the purest sense, are those who identify a need—any need—and fill it. It's a primordial urge, independent of product, service, industry or market.

I believe the most satisfying expression of entrepreneurial activity is one in which the need is felt, explored, defined, a solution is researched, tried and found, and ...finally a gap is closed, a need is met, a solution to a problem is presented. Yes!.... The exhilaration of finding the perfect puzzle piece to snap in place and complete the picture, the final number crunching to complete an algorithm, the new hire who is a perfect fit for your office team, shooting of an arrow that hits a bull's eye on the target, this satisfaction I imagine to be much like that of the charming prince's delegates who placed the glass slipper on Cinderella's tiny foot. Ahhhh, just the right fit.

Is anything so sweet as finding the perfect fit of a solution for a problem?

As a child I watched my Dad invent solutions to problems on a regular basis. It was a way of life for him. The pointed tips of his shirt collar wouldn't lay flat when he dressed for the office. That was unacceptable for a well-dressed man who always wore a suit He located some stiff clear plastic material and cut small strips inserting them through a small slit he made in the material on the underside of his collar to prevent the tips from rolling up. This was long before plastic stays were common in men's dress shirts. His pillow hurt his ear at night, so he bought a thick sheet of foam rubber and cut a hole where his ear would rest alleviating the cramping when he laid down to sleep at night. When he had a problem, he didn't complain about it; he created a solution. He had an entrepreneurial spirit.

Seizing an opportunity is what I love to do. A challenging problem presents an incredible opportunity for ideation, innovation, exploration, solution-bringing, and presenting a new reality. Faced with sluggish systems in a college setting and needing to create corporate training solutions for large companies in my community brought me face to face with a crippling problem our community faced. When I was named the Director of an entrepreneurial learning center charged to meet these needs, I was thrilled with the daunting feat of deriving systems, creating programs, hiring a team, and working against fierce deadlines to launch a new collaboration between industry, college, and the community, but I loved it. I was working in my power alley and worked around the clock to forge a creative and innovative solution in the realm of corporate learning. The solution provided creative learning experiences for operators, engineers, administrators, and managers – over 150,000 training participants were affected with the solutions from this place in just over a decade. Fueled by the desire to fill the huge gaping hole of corporate learning in our community, I took great joy in spearheading a profit center from year one that excelled in our craft. Visitors came from all over the U.S. and abroad to study the creative collaborative effort that seemed to mystify those who had tried and failed.

When I am planning a Leadership Coaching Session, I am driven to find what will work for my individual clients. I am an entrepreneur studying the unique needs of my client, exploring the options and solutions, creating a custom session that will close the gap. The extra hours spent finding the right solution are an investment in not only my client's success, but the satisfaction I derive from watching my clients soar in their leadership exploits. It is palpable—I can taste the savory joy of their success and I'm driven to repeat this time and time again. I've got the bug. I've got the entrepreneurial spirit.

Entrepreneurship is a calling I would say. Seeing the possibilities burns within me and I crave bringing tasty solutions forth! It gives me satisfaction to know I have brought some transformational IMPACT into reality so that the economy is boosted, jobs are created, needs are met, lives are better, and a little part of my destiny has affected the destiny of another.

Gina Inkum CPA Managing Partner, Hoskins & Inkum, LLP

The dictionary defines the entrepreneur as one who manages any enterprise especially a business with considerable initiative and risk. Although there is the tendency to think of entrepreneurs only in terms of business initiatives, to me entrepreneurship transcends beyond business. As an entrepreneur, I am currently operating in the professional services, retail and religious industries. Entrepreneurship is a mindset. It's the ability to think outside the box and being a pacesetter in one's endeavor. It is a mindset required for success in most ventures whether for profit or otherwise. Having the mind of an entrepreneur would make one better at whatever they undertake. An employee with an entrepreneurial spirit would be a stellar employee because his actions are driven with the bottom line in mind. Successful business entrepreneurs are typically leaders wherever they find themselves because, the ability to take initiative and risk permeates every aspect of their lives. It is not surprising that successful business entrepreneurs also play very active roles in their communities and are invaluable assets to society.

I was raised in a family that focused primarily on going to school, getting good grades, getting a high paying job and focusing on climbing the corporate ladder until retirement. My husband on the other hand grew up in family full of entrepreneurs. The mindset of taking risk and initiative was very foreign and took getting use to. The most significant impact in terms of understanding entrepreneurships for me occurred when I read two books by Robert Kiyosaki- Rich Dad, Poor Dad and Retire Young, Retire Rich. These two books gave me a perspective about life which I had not been exposed to prior to the read. The biggest concept is the fact that, a person needs to take responsibility for his life now, or take instructions forever. Understanding the cashflow quadrant and how each group of people leveraged their lives and resources drove home the fact that employees are at the bottom of the chain and if a person really wanted to make significant accomplishments, taking initiative and risk was important. Being a business major, I was familiar with the general concept of the higher the risk, the higher the return however, I had not translated the concept into my career as an individual prior to this exposure.

Entrepreneurship for me means taking responsibility for my life and future. It means, willing to pay the price needed to get myself out of the bottom quadrant. It means understanding that risk is a part of life and inaction in itself is risky because by not taking steps needed to create, we risk being irrelevant and unaccomplished in society which is a risky decision. Entrepreneurship means freedom.

When I found out I was going to be a mom in 2002, the passion to be an entrepreneur grew stronger because I didn't want to be begging all my life. I simply didn't want to be boxed in where I was without freedom to take care of the precious gift. I took 4 years off working in a traditional corporate environment with the restrictions it came with and honed my entrepreneurial skills in that period. Considering, I had never ventured into any risk taking activities prior to that, it was a leap of faith. The words of Robert Kiyosaki rang in my mind daily "take responsibility now or take instructions forever". My husband motivated and allied my fears. In fact, I took my resignation letter to work and returned home without turning it in for several days. My husband would call throughout the day encouraging me to turn it in but the risk factor and fear of loss gripped me. Eventually I mustered the courage to turn it in and when I manager said, we'll keep your position for 6 months, I knew I had become an entrepreneur when I responded

"I'm pretty sure I won't be coming back". It has been an amazing twelve year journey. As an entrepreneur, I have experienced a lot of successes and failures. If I had to do it all over again, I would be an entrepreneur. Entrepreneurship I would say has produced resilience in me that I would never have acquired any other way.

In conclusion, my training as a CPA often fights against the entrepreneurial spirit as CPAs are trained to be risk averse. This however provides the balance needed in making decisions after some form of analysis. Being an entrepreneur has made me a better wife, mother, employee and minister. I dare to say, entrepreneurship has made me better at whatever role I play. My perception in life searches for approaches to accomplishing tasks rather than seeing as impossibilities. There is an element of risk in every aspect of life. Entrepreneurship has equipped me with the ability to analyze very quickly and make decisions required to effectively minimize the risk.

Kaye Caldwell, Author and Entrepreneur

"For all of the most important things, the timing always sucks. Waiting for a good time to quit your job? The stars will never align and the traffic lights of life will never be green at the same time. The universe doesn't conspire against you, but it doesn't go out of its way to line up the pins either.

Conditions are never perfect. "Someday" is a disease that will take your dreams to the grave with you. Pro and con lists are just as bad. If it's important to you and you want to do it, "eventually" just do it…" - Timothy Ferriss

As an emerging entrepreneur and published author, there are two words that capture the essence of what entrepreneurship encapsulates. Faith and perseverance.

I'd always dreamed of writing a book, and becoming a best-selling author whose characters would one day come alive on the big screen. As Timothy Ferriss eloquently stated above, timing was the constant factor that seemed to haunt my dreams and impede the process. Ironically, after 15 years of battling illness (while matriculating through 2 fortune 500 companies); I emerged not only healed, but determined to chart my own course as an entrepreneur and author.

I've learned early on that my desire to take readers on a journey in a way that's never been done before will require subcomponents of perseverance as I delve into unchartered waters to create a magical reading experience like no other. Each component discussed is essential to every creator and nurturer that desires to fill a void or provide a renewed energy to the masses by bringing their business ideas and dreams to fruition.

SEAD (Study, Embrace, Appreciate, Drive)

- Studying the process of other's successes and failures in your industry provides invaluable insight. Time management and strategic planning are often enhanced by learning to avoid the potholes and misfortunes of those that have forged ahead of us. Networking and seeking expertise constantly are daily supplements entrepreneurs can't afford to remove from their diets.

- The ability to embrace challenges and adversity with a resolve to never quit must be the oxygen in the blood of entrepreneurs. The capability to adapt and see obstacles as growing pains instead of sinkholes to failure is the mindset one must not waiver from to survive.

- No idea or company has ever achieved insurmountable success without committed nurturers and dedicated staff. As leaders, it is essential to understand the value of those that labor in the trenches with us. Appreciation is a business strategy that can never be utilized enough.

- Passion is essential, but DRIVE and confidence are the two components that separate those with intentions to pursue their dreams versus entrepreneurs that act on their calling. Entrepreneurship is a way of life. A mere quiet moment for game changers is utilized as an opportunity to envision, inspire, believe, and strategize.

Allow me to share one of my favorite quotes from Jordan Fliegel, CEO of CoachUp.com that beautifully summarizes the necessary tools listed above.

"Entrepreneurship is an unavoidable life calling pursued by those who are fortunate enough to take chances [and are] optimistic enough to believe in themselves, aware enough to see problems around them, stubborn enough to keep going, and bold enough to act again and again. Entrepreneurship is not something you do because you have an idea. It's about having the creativity to question, the strength to believe and the courage to move."

It is my inherent belief that entrepreneurs are equipped with an unwavering faith that epitomizes what the human spirit and resolve is capable of achieving once purpose, faith, and strategic planning intersect. Risk takers don't leap because they are one hundred percent certain of the outcome or landing. They jump because their faith affirms that no matter the landing; they are intrinsically equipped with greatness that will allow them to rebound.

Optimists without a strategy are mere day dreamers. Entrepreneurs are dreamers that see beyond the scope of impossible equipped with knowledge and a perseverance unbridled by an expiration date.

ENTREPRENUERSHIP A MINDSET NOT A STOREFRONT

Scott Chevalier CEO of Power House Youth Project

I cannot tell you how many times I have someone, in the middle of our conversation, state their desire to start their own business. It normally is initiated by a previous conversation that I have had with them about a new business venture or something else I am exploring. It seems to ignite a passion that was dwindling in them from their daily routine.

It is in those moments that I begin to challenge their mindset. I don't ask them how much money they have to invest, what their marketing plan is for their product or service, or ask them about their small business structure. Those questions can be answered and worked out in the process. I am more interested in their perspective of business and those of us who call ourselves entrepreneurs. I find there is a large gap in the mindset of those who move on their passion and those who are moved by others passions. It's not what they hear, but what happens between their ears that really matters. Let me explain.

Recently I had the opportunity to speak at a local high school on career day. This was a day set aside for the under classmen - to give them opportunities to evaluate potential careers and ask questions of those who are in the working force. My session was a large general session, so I focused my attention on a broad stroke and not just a single career path. The entrepreneur uses a GPS with many routes in order to achieve their goals and it was my goal in this session to challenge the single mindedness that had been fed to them during most of their school lives. It started with a video clip from one of my family's favorite TV shows, "The Middle". Axl, their oldest son, is struggling to find direction and is having a conversation with a concrete statue as he is locked in the library. All of the influences and voices in his life had been erased and it was just himself and his thoughts conversing with his imaginary masonry friend about life after high school. He struggles to put it into words and then as if summarizing for a paper he states, "I'm just not sure my awesomeness will transfer into the real world and I'm scared." There it is…the core root of anyone who wants to be an entrepreneur…FEAR. What if I fail? What if it's a stupid idea? What if no one buys it? What if I succeed? Fear grabs us between the ears and whispers all the "what if's" we can handle.

After the video clip, I made this statement to over 500 freshmen looking for direction. "Your awesomeness will not transfer and it is OK to not know what you want to do right now!"

70% of Americans today are not satisfied with their daily jobs and many will spend a lifetime changing jobs over ten times to try and find the right path. (2014 Gallup Poll)

We are told our whole lives what to do; go to the elementary school, then middle school, then high school and then college and then…someone fill in the blank. Unfortunately, the cultures GPS system has not been updated in quite some time and we get lost and disillusioned thinking that a piece of paper and a load of debt will deliver us to the Promised Land with a great career. Today in the United States 8 out of 10 students with a bachelor's degree are working at fast food restaurants and 1/3 of all PhD students are on food stamps. (Gallup Poll 2014) What happened to this plan for my future? We need an update to our GPS system to find the right path.

In my local paper on the front page of the business section it read, "Over 53% of CEO's are dissatisfied with the candidates that the colleges are producing." The reason is simple, it's their "state of mind". They have depended on the piece of paper and a class that most likely is being led by someone who has never been out of the classroom. (Tennessean, April 27, 2014)

When we look at our future, all too often, we ask the wrong questions. We ask, "What should I study?" and "Where should I go to school?" Perhaps we need to adjust our mindset and ask ourselves these questions: "Do I need to go to school?" "What path can get me to my goal?" "Who can help me achieve my dream?" If we stop relying on a syllabus and an archaic system, we may avoid debt and confusion and begin a journey marked with thrills and adventure. That does not mean it will be easy, but it does mean I get to pursue what fills my tank.

If we fail to learn this lesson, we enter the game of redundancy. We go to college, acquire student loan debt and graduate with a piece of paper hoping to find a job. It is then we find out that our loans must be paid back. So, we enter a JOB to pay a BILL and find it very difficult to get off the ride day after day, week after week, and year after year. Until eventually, we run into someone who runs their own business and they re-ignite our dream and passion. We ask, "How did you get into business for yourself?" The answer is very simple…"I changed my mindset."

Some of the best practical steps you can take to change your mindset are listed below. They have taken me very far on my journey and I continue to rely on them today.

1. Avoid SNIOPS: This is the Sudden Negative Influence of Other People. These dream snatchers spend a lifetime telling you why it cannot be done and often plant seeds of fear in your heart by creating a field of doubt around you.

2. VISION: Have a vision of where you are headed. Simply begin to see yourself in 5, 10, and 20 years doing what ignites you and envision what that looks like. I am a firm believer in the vision being the life for your journey. Without it, your journey will perish and end much too quickly.

3. PERSERVERANCE: The life of an entrepreneur, although it can be very fulfilling, will have days of fatigue and stress. You will want to surrender your dream to the 9-5 job by looking at someone else's security and constant paycheck. You will have to overcome your own doubt and insecurities and learn to bunker down for the long run. Write down the small victories when they occur so you have lines in the sand where victory took place. You may need to re-visit them at points on your journey. There are many in history that were told they could not make it. Walt Disney was fired from a local paper for 'lacking imagination.' Michael Jordan was cut from his high school basketball

team. Albert Einstein did not speak until age 4 and was told by his teachers he would not amount to much. And, Oprah Winfrey was demoted from her news anchor job because she was 'not fit for TV'. (www.onlinecollege.org)

It is here that I must reveal the true secret to these 3 steps. It is my FAITH. I find, in my personal walk with Jesus Christ, an understanding that HE has a plan for me and it is my job while on earth to accomplish that task and not simply work to earn a paycheck. I continue to PUSH in the rough times knowing that someone beyond my abilities causes kingdoms to rise and fall, and enables the sun to rise and fall. When the road gets weary I PUSH. Pray Until Something Happens. Connect to the God of the universe and join Him for the ride.

Imagine, if I could have revealed that last part to the class in the high school that day. It may have set off an avalanche of dreamers, builders, creators, and entrepreneurs who could change the world and not simply take a job.

ENTREPRENUERSHIP A MINDSET NOT A STOREFRONT

CEO of Konadu Body, Jennifer McGill

Entrepreneurship is the ability to discover the need for something, and taking a big step forward to create that "something" to satisfy that need. It is when you take a big risk to manufacture a product or create a service that can help make someone else's life easy or better. An entrepreneur must have certain characteristics that sets him or her apart from the rest. That is because the journey of entrepreneurship is not always smooth, fun and easy. There are a lot of puzzles pieces to find and put together over time, pitfalls, hurdles, problem solving, failures, loneliness and issues to deal with. For this reason not everybody is cut out to be an entrepreneur. To me the four key characteristics of true and successful entrepreneurs are listed in the paragraphs below.

Determined & Motivated:

An Entrepreneur must be determined and motivated to achieve their goal. There are a lot of things that may or may not work out in the life of an entrepreneur. For example, an idea that seemed brilliant at conception in your mind, may turn out to be not so brilliant when finally implemented. It can be discouraging when you spend several hours, days or months creating something, only to fail in the end. Only those who are willing to work through, and learn from their mistakes or failures, and try again, until they achieve their goals are cut out for entrepreneurship. In entrepreneurship, those who are determined to go all the way no matter the cost or obstacles will eventually see the fruits of their labor.

Unique & Creative Thinking:

As an entrepreneur, chances are you are thinking of doing something that may already exist, or provide a service that is already being provided by someone else. Your ability to think creatively and uniquely about what you have to offer and how best to satisfy the need of your market, will set you apart. Entrepreneurs, who are always able to figure out a unique, creative and competitive way of offering a service or product are the most successful.

Risk Taker and Not Afraid of Failure:
Most entrepreneurs are risk-takers. Our motivation for taking risks is discovering a need out there, and determining how to satisfy that need.

We are moved to implement an idea we've had for a long time, manufacture a product, or provide a service without knowing what the true outcome is going to be. We are not guaranteed success, we just happen to believe in our ideas so much so that, we take a leap of faith. Really that is what entrepreneurship is all about, taking a leap of faith and believing that after all the preparation and research we have done, we have a good chance of succeeding. On the other side, if it turns out to not work out the way we expect, we do not give up. We keep trying until success shows up. It may not be the same thing we started with, it could be a completely different idea or product we discover as a result of our failures. All the same determined entrepreneurs are not afraid to take risks, they expect failures along the way, but they do not let those failures hold them down, they keep at it until they succeed.

Believe Strongly In Their Ideas:
The journey of entrepreneurship can be very rewarding but it is not always smooth. Those who believe in what they have to offer will do whatever it takes to weather all the storms that come along with entrepreneurship, until they reach their destination of success. The degree to which you believe that what you have to offer can change lives or make people's lives easier or better usually has a great impact on the level of determination, competitiveness, passion, excitement and

risk an entrepreneur is willing to take to achieve success.

So what does entrepreneurship mean to me? Entrepreneurship is an act of leadership, a calling to bring brilliant ideas, services, or products into the market place for the betterment of society. It is the desire, determination, motivation and the ability to take a huge or small risk to create something that can impact the world in a unique and effective way. It is believing that you were created to do something that only you can do it the way you are planning on doing it. It is taking a leap of faith and stepping into the space that God has created for you, to use your unique talents and gifts to create something valuable that can transform and change lives for the better.

Entrepreneurship is a mindset that enables you to open your eyes, to identify opportunities all around you, tapping into your area of your expertise, and using those opportunities to create products and services that can be hugely profitable to society and to you as well. It is waking up every day and having the passion and motivation to keep doing what you started regardless of the tough times, or obstacles, even if no one sees the potential for your success. It is knowing that you are mostly all alone in this journey, and responsible for every aspect of the business. It is doing effective and efficient multitasking, and enjoying the independence, responsibilities, and successes that that comes with running your own business or organization.

Christina Sheer is a Social Media Evangelist

The founder of Sheer Goodness, a digital branding agency that provides social media services and digital brand coaching. Her vision is to shine light on the good brands do by helping them build their brand, define their goals and create their action plan. Her 12+ years of business management experience in the areas of entertainment, tourism and marketing has provided her with the necessary tools to consultant with small businesses, churches, entertainment industry professionals, non-profit organizations and entrepreneurs around the world. In 2015, she released her debut book "Missionary On The Go: A 30-Day Devotional for World Changers." Currently, she is living in Cape Town, South Africa where she serves as a missionary and communications coordinator for a church.

3 Keys to Brand Success

As an entrepreneur for more than twelve years it is my joy to share with you my keys to brand success. In an always evolving world, I have found that in order to be a successful business person I have always utilized the three keys of technology, tools and teachings to find brand success as an entrepreneur.

I like to envision that each and every one of our brands are a vehicle that we drive on the highway to destiny. In order for the vehicle to start it requires a key whether you are an aspiring business owner or currently running a thriving brand to drive you to your next entrepreneurial milestone.

When we are driving along sometimes we can get stressed out or frustrated by those around us or even difficult environmental conditions. Imagine having road rage but towards your brand! Scary thought, but the truth is we all have experienced frustration as an entrepreneur. That's why as a brand on the highway of destiny you need to be very aware of our mindset. In order to get to your final destination you need to have an early adopter entrepreneurial mindset.

Before we dive into the three keys to brand success let's talk about what it takes to be an early adopter. An early adopter is a person who starts using a product or technology as soon as it becomes available. They are eager to explore new things but risk taking is low on their priority list. They love coming up with new ideas and founding businesses.

Who are early adopters? They are the innovators. They are the pioneers. They are the few people willing to jump off the cliff in faith that they will fly. If you are reading this book, then this is probably you or you have an early adopter / entrepreneurial mindset when it comes to business. Now, let's equip you with the three keys of brand success!

Technology // The application of knowledge for a practical purpose.

As an entrepreneur technology is a vital key to your success. It today's digital world using the Internet, social media and mobile solutions will set you apart for the competition. The major mindset challenge with technology entrepreneurs need to overcome is the frustrations that comes along with as soon as you master one aspect of a product / service another is released (sometimes that does the same task more efficiently). There is quite a learning curve but that's where the early adopter mindset comes in handy when embracing technology in your brand strategy.

As a business owner you have the opportunity to pioneer

technology early on taking advantage of the fruits of the new resource, establishing yourself as a thought leader and developing a new skillset that others want to follow. If you are entrepreneurially minded you will quickly realize the open door this presents to monetize your new skills by establishing yourself as a teacher / coach in the marketplace. As you embrace each new technological advancement you will find yourself surrounded by potential clients seeking you as well as the product / service you are using to achieve success.

Also, I want to note that technology is an essential resource to ensuring you achieve maximum productivity. Make sure that as you continue to embrace technology it has a practical purpose and ultimately moves you closer to your objective.

Tools To be equipped with device for production.

I love the definition of tools because it brings great clarity and focus as to why you would want to embrace them as a key to success for your brand. Entrepreneurs all over the world are looking for (and creating) tools to make life easier, more productive, efficient, etc. You need help with something ... there probably is a tool to help you achieve it. If not, well you may have just converted an excellent business idea.

Today, I want to focus on the tools you can use to excel on the highway to destiny. There are some incredible time management and team communication tools you
can utilize to ensure your brand is well on it's way to success. Below is my ABCs of tools!

Asana - task management

Basecamp - project collaboration

Canva - graphic design tool

ENTREPRENUERSHIP A MINDSET NOT A STOREFRONT

Dropbox - online storage

Evernote - note taking

Fiverr - freelance marketplace
Google Drive - cloud storage & data backup

Hootsuite - social media management

Infusionsoft - crm software

Jot - app for consolidating emails to send to yourself

Kickstarter - crowd funding platform

Linkedin - social network, lead generation

Mailchimp - email marketing

Notability - note taker app

Overcast - podcast player

PicMonkey - photo editing app

QR Reader - mobile app for scanning QR bar codes
Regram - instagram reposting app

Shopify - online store

Themeforest - professional wordpress website templates

Uber - private driver app

Videoshop - video editing app

Wordswap - typography app

Xero - online invoicing

YouNeedABudget.com - budgeting software

Zapier - automate your work processes

Teachings // An idea or principle taught by an expert.

An entrepreneur that aspires to embrace technology and implement the use of innovative tools in their life will find themselves seeking teachings to assist them with achieving their new level of brand success. Entrepreneurs typically have extremely busy schedules and find themselves multitasking however they lack the time and energy needed to spend hours learning a new technology or tool. Ultimately, these are the thought leaders looking for a timesaving route on their highway to destiny. Hence, the vital need for coaches and teachers in every aspect of the marketplace.

I love the fact that teachings are an idea or principle taught by an expert! Entrepreneurs know that their time is a valuable resource. This is why they seek out someone with experience and wisdom so they can glean from their knowledge. Why spend 10,000 hours learning a skill when you can purchase or a book or an online coaching program to learn how to accomplish the same task from a seasoned professional? As an entrepreneur time and time again you will find yourself with the need to learn a new skill so be sure to keep in mind is this something you need to learn on your own or is is time to seek a skilled professional to coach you on the path to brand success.

Personally, Udemy, Skillshare and Lynda are my favorite online platforms for obtaining teachings resources. YouTube is a great (and free) option too. Regardless of where you obtain your teachings, the important take away is that in order to be a successful entrepreneur you will need to continue to learn new skills to thrive in your career!

In short, here is my formula for fulfilling your brand's destiny:

Early Adopter Mindset
 + 3 Keys To Brand Success (Technology, Tools, Teachings)
 = A Destiny Fulfilled

From person to person the order of implementing these keys will vary but know that each one used strategically at the right time will provide you with the roaring engine you need to get to your next destination. As you adopt and implement these three keys in your brand watch and see the door of opportunity open as you pursue entrepreneurial success.

Chapter 4
Benefits of Networking for Entrepreneurs

After attending many networking events for many years, I realized that networking is one of the most valuable uses of my time in terms of return—and not just in monetary terms. Most networking events are free. It's full of like-minded individuals, and if you go to the right events, it's full of people that you can work with or learn from in some way.

Be careful about just attending events where people are only trying to sell you something. Most of these social networking events provide a laid back atmosphere to have conversations with similar people, and these informal events often lead to many opportunities and potential ways you can work together.

Face-to-face networking events are better because they create lasting impressions in the your mind and in the minds of people you meet. I mean, ultimately, it's not about whom you know, but rather who knows you, right? Try to also attend events that aren't necessarily tied to your area of expertise.

I have attended meeting with engineers, technology gurus, accountants and many other industries networking groups. Why? I have seen these groups be very beneficial because it makes me think outside of the box and learn how others can be a benefit to me and how I can be one for them as well. I have partnered with several of them and it was a great collaboration for my clients and for me.

This can always lead to future opportunities for both parties, in terms of help, advice and business. It can also motivate you go further, take the plunge into adding other services or products because of your different industry connections and knowledge.

After networking events, make sure to stay connected with those that you meet. Take a look at the business cards you received and email those people about what you spoke about while it is still fresh in your mind. You may feel you are too busy to attend these events, but they act as a nice break from being stuck in front of a computer. And sometimes they can count as being at work because you are inevitably spreading the name of your business across an audience that can add value to your business—and it's a great chance to learn something and get ideas. You will see the value in forming and maintaining a strong contact base, which will serve you well for years to come.

There are many strong startup communities around the world now, and in times of economic uncertainty I truly believe that startup communities help you in the progress building your business in a phase of business growth that can be challenging for many.

There will be times when you may need help or advice, and you will want to have built a strong network. "Your net worth is only as good as your network".

FIVE BENEFITS OF NETWORKING

Small business is all about networking, building relationships and taking action.

Shared Knowledge

Networking is great for sharing ideas and knowledge. Whether it's asking for feedback or discussing your point of view on new idea or concept.

Opportunities

It's given that networking will result in opportunities. You have to continue to do it because you don't know when it will happen. I referral from networking event could lead to new contract or funding.

You have to be seen in order for the opportunities to come your way.

Connections

Remember you are not just gaining exposure to the people in the room, you are building connections with their network too. And remember it's not just a one-way street. When you have something to offer as well it makes the connection more value with an increase on your Return on your Investment of time and money.

Increased Confidence

By regularly networking, and pushing yourself to talk to people you don't know, it will help increase your confidence. As you grow your business you will continue to see how important this skill is to business growth.

Raising Your Profile

Being visible and getting noticed is a big benefit of networking. By attending business and social events, people will begin to recognize you. This will help to build your reputation as a knowledgeable, person or expert in your business area as you continue to offer useful information or tips those who need it. When a need comes up and it's your area you want them to remember you. Most of my referrals typically comes this way for my business services.

Building a business can be very hard and challenging, especially if you're in it alone. Building a network of friends, professionals, and other like-minded individuals will prove to be useful every step of the way as operate on a day-to-day basis.

Confidence and motivation can be gained from others in your network, and you may even find unique opportunities that are difficult to discover elsewhere, such as partnership, employee, or investor opportunities. Make networking an ongoing practice. You will see the great benefits as you continue to engage in the opportunities that come to you to network.

ARE YOU A DOOR OPENER?

There have been many people that have opened doors for me. This is another form of networking and helping other move forward. By doing this I know many more doors will be opened for me as well. I feel honored when I am able to do the same. Who are you supposed to open a door for? It's not just about you making it, but about helping someone else do the same.

Happiness often sneaks in through a door you didn't know you left open. ~ John Barrymore

Great leadership is not about being in charge of people, it's about helping people go to the next level. Part of that is opening doors for people when we can and should. Sometimes people who had doors opened for them forget that they should reach back and help the next person. Don't forget LEADERSHIP is also about opening doors for others.

"Be an opener of doors" ~ Ralph Waldo Emerson

Chapter 5
Common Characteristics of Successful Entrepreneurs

Entrepreneurship is the process of starting a business, typically a startup company offering an innovative product, process or service.

RISK-TAKER
- Takes on challenges, highly optimistic, and rational about decision making

BUSINESS FOCUS
- A focus on metrics, goals that align to business mission and vision
- Action oriented focused on results

CREATIVE THINKER
- Thinks past boundaries.
- Generates ideas and explores new ways of doing old things.

PROMOTER
- Speaks boldly about the business and understand company vision

RELATIONSHIP BUILDER
- Has a high social awareness.
- When building relationships looks for mutually beneficial opportunities.
- Understands as you help others solve problems and complete projects your business grows.

KNOWLEDGE SEEKER
- Knows the benefit of being a lifelong learner.
- Understand the importance of spending time studying areas of expertise by reading books, attending seminars and hiring a coach.

STRATEGIC
- Looks at all of the approaches to making a project or product successful.
- Takes into consideration that there are risk and

Not all entrepreneurs are created the same. They come from different backgrounds and geographic locations, income brackets and social classes, as well as education levels. One thing is consistent and that is successful entrepreneurs all possess some of the same traits.

Full of Determination

When you set out to become an entrepreneur it will require you to set very clear goals along the way. If you aren't fully determined to make it there is a good chance you will fall under the pressure.

Not afraid of risks

Some of the most successful entrepreneurs took major risks, and they paid off in a big way. Shark Tank's Barbara Corcoran turned a $1,000 loan into a $5 billion-dollar real estate business that she sold for $66 million back in 2001.

Have a High level of Confidence

Entrepreneurs that have a high level of confidence are able to get the job done even under the most stressful conditions. When challenges come, a successful entrepreneur focuses on the finish line and the end reward.

Craves Learning ~ Life Long Learner

You have to stay sharp, and that requires that you are a lifelong learner. Industries constantly change and evolve and only those that are also growing through constant learning will stay ahead.

Understands failure is Part of the Game

Richard Branson said it best: *"Few first ventures work out. It is how a beginning entrepreneur deals with failure that sets that person apart. In fact, failure is one of the secrets to success, since some of the best ideas arise from the ashes of a shuttered business."*

Passionate about his or her business

Passion fuels the drive and determination required to be successful, whether you are building a company from the ground up or buying a franchise that already had a track record of success.

Chapter 6
Successful Entrepreneurs

Rising to the level of a successful entrepreneur requires creating and following a successful business strategy while focusing on making a difference instead of making money. Entrepreneurs also set standards of high quality. Being an industry leader and developing strategic partnerships can be key factors to business success as well. They have the mindset that is focused. Mindset is the established set of attitudes held by someone.

Successful entrepreneurs often find a viable example to follow when they wish to start a business in a particular industry. They study the strategies of successful businesses already doing what they wish to do and incorporate the best strategies into their own. A lot of useful information can be gathered by tweaking it to fit your company's process. It is better to focus on working on something meaningful by making a difference in the lives of customers. Such meaningful work often leads to success.

The difference between success and failure is sometimes determined by how much an entrepreneur values quality, integrity and innovation. Top entrepreneurs understand that they must seek out quality people to work with and produce high-quality products that impress their target market. Quality helps to drive sales, which leads to business growth. Many business leaders focus on promoting a personal brand by publishing useful content and sharing success stories, which establishes their position as industry thought leaders. Listed below are a few of the top entrepreneurs.

Coco Chanel
"Success is often achieved by those who don't know that failure is

inevitable."

Coco Chanel was born in 1883 to an unmarried mother who worked as a laundry woman in a charity hospital. Her father was an itinerant street vendor who peddled work clothes. She lived an entirely unglamorous life. She learned to sew at age six and was able to find employment as a seamstress. Perhaps her own story inspired her quote. "Success has nothing to do with what you gain in life or accomplish for yourself. It's what you do for others."

Danny Thomas once referred to himself as a "starving actor," and vowed that if he found success, he would open a shrine dedicated to St. Jude Thaddeus, the patron saint of hopeless causes. The actor became successful and was best known for his television sitcom Make Room for Daddy, but he never forgot his promise. In the 1950s he and his wife traveled the U.S. to raise funds to build the St. Jude Children's Research Hospital.

Booker T. Washington
"Success isn't measured by the position you reach in life; it's measured by the obstacles you overcome."

Booker T. Washington was born in slavery in 1856. After being freed by the Emancipation Proclamation he moved with his family to West Virginia. He became ae became a prominent national leader for African Americans and a leading voice for former slaves and their descendants.

Babe Ruth
"Never let the fear of striking out get in your way."
Ruth rose above his humble beginnings, inspired thousands and became one of the greatest baseball players of all time.

When you own your own business, you may sometimes feel that you will never make it. These people most likely felt the same way, but they persevered to create legacies that last throughout time. Start small and begin your journey to success by making a positive impact in your community or industry.

Billionaire Mark Cuban: There are no shortcuts.

The investor and owner of the Dallas Mavericks tells Business Insider the best advice he ever got was: "Do the work. Out-work. Out-think. Out-sell your expectations. There are no shortcuts." The advice came from his father, who did upholstery on cars, when Cuban was in high school. "He was always very encouraging but also realistic," Cuban says of his dad.

Restaurateur Jon Taffer

"Years ago when I was very young," recalls Taffer, the host of TV show "Bar Rescue" and a former business owner, in a recent interview with Business Insider, "a VP of Hyatt looked at me and said, 'You look, but you don't see.'" Taffer learned to look not just at the big picture, but also at every place setting, light fixture, and customer exchange. "See every crack, every detail. I learned to really see and not just look at my business," he says.

FUBU founder Daymond John: Don't chase the money.

When he was growing up, John's mother said, "Money is a great slave but a horrible master."

"In the earlier days, I was really doing things because I thought what I wanted was to be rich," the "Shark Tank" investor tells Business Insider's Richard Feloni. "For the most part, those businesses failed, and then later when I started doing something casually because I loved it, that business burst."

Panera Bread founder and CEO Ron Shaich: Competitive advantage is everything.

"Losing competitive advantage is the greatest risk in business," Shaich tells Business Insider. If you don't have a reason for people to walk past your competitors and come to your business, he says, then you don't exist.

Real estate mogul Barbara Corcoran: My best advice was an insult.

Call it reverse psychology, but it was an insult that motivated Corcoran to succeed. "It's kind of weird. The best advice was the worst advice," she told Business Insider's Henry Blodget. "It was from my boyfriend and partner in my first business when he told me I would never succeed without him. I was injured no doubt. But thank God he insulted me because I would not have built a big business without that.

Dilbert creator Scott Adams: Don't give up.
"The best advice I got was before I was a syndicated cartoonist," Adams tells Business Insider. "I asked advice of a professional cartoonist, Jack Cassady, who had a TV show called 'Funny Business' years ago on PBS. I wrote to him, and he gave me this advice: 'It's a competitive business, but don't give up.'"

The Container Store founder and CEO Kip Tindell: "Business should be a win-win for everyone".

One of Tindell's favorite lessons comes from industrialist Andrew Carnegie, who said: "Fill the other guy's basket to the brim. Making money then becomes an easy proposition."

Lululemon founder Chip Wilson: It's OK to ask for help.
"It took me a long time to understand it, but [the advice was] to ask for help and that I don't know it all," Wilson tells Business Insider. "People love to help. I don't have to be insecure and know it all."

Entrepreneur and author Tim Ferriss: You are who you associate with.

"The best advice I ever got is: You're the average of the five people you associate with the most," Ferriss, author of the best-selling book "The 4-Hour Workweek,"

Camping World CEO Marcus Lemonis: Get into a business where you can be a big fish.

"The best advice I ever got was from Lee Iaccoca, who was very influential in my career,"

Advertising entrepreneur Sara Rotman: Being comfortable is the enemy.

"The best advice I ever received was from my first accountant when I was discussing the launch of my company," says Rotman, founder of ad agency MODCo, which has clients like Vera Wang, True Religion, and Tory Burch.

"We were speaking about my business plan and how much money to borrow to launch. She wisely said, 'Only have enough cash on hand to barely survive; never so much that you are comfortable. It's important to stay scared in the beginning.'"

5 Acre Farms CEO Dan Horan: Simplicity is everything.

"Simplicity is really important," "It's got to be simple, and sometimes to make something simple you have to really, really study everything about it.

Hello Design CEO David Lai: Your time is a precious commodity.

"When I was growing up my father would always tell me, 'We all only have 24 hours a day. It's what we choose to do with that time that defines us,'"

NewsCred CEO Shafqat Islam: If you're not being told 'no' constantly, you're not pushing hard enough.

"Multiple people have told me this, and I don't know if I can credit it to a single person, but one thing that I think about is if you're not getting told 'no' enough times a day, you're probably not doing it right, or you're probably not pushing yourself hard enough".

SumAll CEO Dane Atkinson: Learn to say 'no' and focus on what you do best.

"One thing that I've slowly come to realize is that focus is so critically important," "Saying 'no' to great ideas is necessary to get to the brilliant ones.

Chapter 7
Social Entrepreneurship

A **social enterprise** is an organization that applies commercial strategies to maximize improvements in human and environmental well-being - this may include maximizing social impact rather than profits for external shareholders. Social enterprises can be structured as a for-profit or non-profit, and may take the form (depending in which country the entity exists and the legal forms available) of a co-operative, mutual organization, a disregarded entity, a social business, a benefit corporation a community interest company or a charitable organization.

1) Articulate a problem *and* a solution

As an social entrepreneur, you need to convince people to trust you—to fund you, to invest their time, to leave better paying jobs to support your cause. "You need to clearly articulate a problem *and* the solution,

2) Surround yourself with experts in your field

Spend time or study people who are doing what you want to do very well and are considered an experts in the field.

3) Hire staff that's flexible and entrepreneurial

If you're running a start-up organization, you need to run with people who think entrepreneurially. People with the entrepreneurial mindset will stick around longer than those that just see it has a job or volunteer opportunity.

4) Be able to measure your impact

Make sure you can track and measure what you are doing. Data analysis is very important when sharing the vision and outcomes with donors and volunteers.

Social Enterprise Spotlight

Esther continues to be an exemplary student and business owner as well as a person of tremendous character with significant leadership skills. She has taken on many volunteer activities and understands the importance of serving and the impact it makes. She continues to be passionate about giving back and being a difference maker for her generation. She is currently a freshman at NYU School of Engineering majoring in Chemical and Biomolecular Engineering. Her enthusiasm and energy have been matched over the years with a discipline that is remarkable for someone her age. Her discipline is a commitment to learning and excellence. She has held many leadership roles in her school and community such as student government vice president, member of the national science honor society, member of Nashville Tennessee Mayor Karl Dean youth council, and Bank of America student leader intern. She continues to participate in various leadership roles at NYU.

Last year, I was impressed as she engaged me in a discussion about poverty and doing something to make an impact locally and internationally. She not only talked about it she began to do something about it by assisting in raising funds to support children and families in the 3rd world country of DRC, Congo. After a strategy meeting with me she put together a plan coordinating a sewing machine project, so the women could start a small business making purses and clothes. After her projects in the Congo she launched her on social enterprise www.EstherNzuzi.com that continues support humanitarian efforts in DRC Congo.

A new generation of entrepreneurs are, creating new products and services that will change the world. They want to have a great profitable business, but they also want to make a big impact that will change the world. Esther Nzuzi hires women in the DRC Congo to assist with the production of the products.

Esther's mission in life is to help youth develop an appreciation for themselves in a way that they may cultivate a creative mind, pure soul, and skilled hands. As a result, each may flourish into the ability to inspire, train, and empower others. To achieve this goal, Esther created *Esther Nzuzi LLC*.

Currently *Esther Nzuzi* sells African inspired bags. The cross shoulder bags are known for its convenient, comfortable, and colorful style. They serve as a perfect gift; the bags can be used for anything from a dance bag to a casual hanging-out-with-friends bag. The lightweight bags are big enough to store anything from shoes to sweaters to books to makeup. Check out the purses at www.esthernzuzi.com

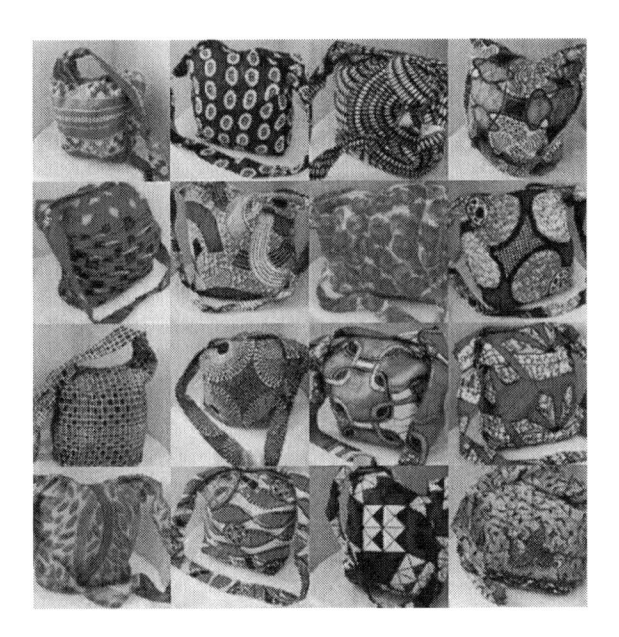

Esther Nzuzi works directly with Luila Village Ministries, a 501(c) non-profit that aims to empower women, educate children, and spread the gospel in Luila, Democratic Republic of Congo and surrounding villages. A percentage of all profits received from each sale at *Esther Nzuzi* will be given to Luila Village Ministries. You may stay updated with Luila Village Ministries by following them on Facebook.

ENTREPRENUERSHIP A MINDSET NOT A STOREFRONT

esthernzuzi.com

CHAPTER 8
Leadership Principles for Entrepreneurs

Creating and building a business is not a one-man show. It requires a team effort, or at least the ability to build trust and confidence among key players, and effectively communicate with partners, team members, investors, vendors, and customers. These actions are the hallmark of an effective leader.

Behind the actions are a set of principles and characteristics that entrepreneurial leaders, like Bill Gates and Steve Jobs, seem to have in common. Look for these and nurture them in your own context to improve the odds of success for your own startup:

1. Clarity of vision and expectations. You must be able and willing to communicate to everyone your vision, goals, and objectives. Just as importantly, you have to be absolutely clear about who you are, what you stand for, and what you expect from everyone around you. People won't follow you if they are in the dark or confused.

2. Willingness to make decisions. It is often said that making any decision is better than making no decision. Even better than "any decision" is a good decision made quickly. Business decisions always involve risk, at times a great deal of it. Smart entrepreneurs always balance the risk with facts, when they have them, rather than their gut.

3. Experience and knowledge in your business area. Effective leaders set a personal standard of competence for every person and function in the startup. It must be clear that you have the knowledge, insight, and skill to make your new company better than your very best competitor.

4. Commitment and conviction for the venture. This commitment must be passionate enough to motivate and inspire people to do their best work, and put their heart into the effort. Behind the passion must be a business model that makes sense in today's world, and a determination to keep going despite setbacks.

5. Open to new ideas and creativity. In business, this means spending time and resources on new ideas, as well as encouraging people to find faster, better, cheaper, and easier ways to produce results, beat competition, and improve customer service. Be a role model and guide others to excel.

6. Courage to acknowledge and attack constraints. An effective leader is willing and able to allocate resources to remove obstacles to the success of the startup, as well as removing constraints on individuals on the team. It is believing that where there is the will, there will be a way.

7. Reward continuous learning. You have to encourage everyone to learn and grow as a normal and natural part of business. That means no punishment for failures, and positive opportunities for training and advancement. Personally, it means upgrading your own skills, listening, and reading about new developments and approaches.

8. Self-discipline for consistency and reliability. An effective leader is totally predictable, calm, positive, and confident, even under pressure. People like to follow someone when they don't have to "walk on

eggshells" to avoid angry outbursts, or assume daily changes in direction.

9. Accept responsibility for all actions. Everyone and every company makes mistakes. Good entrepreneurs don't want to be seen as perfect, and they have to be seen as willing to accept the fact that "the buck stops here." No excuses, or putting the blame on the economy, competitors, or team members.

The good news is that all of these principles of leadership are learnable. The bad news is that it's not easy. Don't assume that success as an entrepreneur is only about great presentations, killing competitors, or having insanely great ideas. It's really more about leadership, understanding the needs of your prospective clients, and communicating your solutions with clarity.

Leadership Principles from Nehemiah for Entrepreneurs

Restoration for your Business or Idea

Evidence of this is seen in how Nehemiah reacted when he heard that the city walls had been torn down and that the gates had been burnt with fire. Nehemiah responded with mourning, fasting, and prayer (1:4). Even though the people living in Jerusalem had been allowed to return to their city and managed to rebuild a temple, they had now been there for 80 years and still had not rebuilt the walls around the city. Don't get stuck with seeing the business or idea as too hard or challenging to achieve. Move forward even with the unknowns because that's when you see progress

Prayer Strategy

Eleven different prayers are mentioned in the book of Nehemiah. In these prayers Nehemiah shared his burden and responsibility with God, and God answered in the end. Therefore "these prayers are an encouragement to all readers to follow the example of Nehemiah, for prayer brings God's power to bear on the difficult situations in life. Start the year off with a prayer strategy. We know when we have a plan or strategy that we are following we see things happen. The prayer strategy and focus will do the same thing.

Communicate your vision as a solution to a problem that must be addressed immediately.

The idea of rebuilding the walls proposed by Nehemiah is a solution to a problem which the people have faced for the past 80 years since they first returned to Jerusalem from exile. Nehemiah shared a vision that was of God and was a solution to a problem. What problem or solution are you addressing with your business? In order to determine what this may be you will need to write the vision down and identify why it is needed.

"Protect your organization's core and culture with a thick wall built by people who not only want to save their own skin."

In the book of Nehemiah, the people were not trying to save their own skin. They were trying to rebuild their city and return to faithful worship of God. Build a core team that wants to see the business grow and impact others. It is okay to want to be successful, but it is not good when it is at the level of hurting or stepping on other people to get there. When the team works together everyone wins. That's why TEAM = Together Everyone Achieves More

"A leader need not do all the planning, yet he must assure that the planning gets done."

For years they knew that they needed to get the walls rebuilt around the city. Nehemiah arrived and displayed the extensiveness of effort that it took to rebuild the walls. When you empower your team they will get the work done. When you micro manage them they will not move forward with their creative innovative ideas because they are waiting on you. Put the plan together and allow them to soar.

Chapter 9
Negotiations and Business Pitch

Competition is at the heart of business. Companies try to outperform each other, outsell each other, and even destroy each other. It's the nature of the game. But cooperation has its place to. Companies often work together to achieve mutual aims. They form partnerships, using their different assets and strengths to become an even greater competitive force.

But a good partnership is tough to build. Any kind of agreement has to make sense for both sides, and each will try to get as much out of a deal as possible. Sure, they're cooperating, but they want to make sure they're cooperating in the best possible way for themselves.

So how does a strategic partnership begin? Well, any agreement begins with a negotiation, a strategic negotiation. And how does a negotiation begin? It begins with an idea, an idea for two companies to work together.

When you pitch an idea for a strategic partnership, there are several key techniques you'll need. This includes broaching the topic, pitching the basic idea, and speculating about feasibility. It also includes showing tentative agreement, outlining how the partnership might work, and outlining the next steps in the process.

When your business has no revenue and you have very little negotiating leverage beyond the power of your business idea, the traditional rules of negotiation just don't apply.

Negotiating With Employees

Your employees and consultants will be faced with a need for more money and will knock on your door to negotiate a better deal. How should you handle this situation?

First, you should always be respectful of the personal needs of your employees. In a small startup that's resource-constrained, employees' personal lives and professional lives are particularly intertwined. This doesn't mean giving employees a raise if they ask for it, but it does mean listening carefully to the reason for their request for more money. In many cases, they may not need more money but simply more flex time, more vacation, more upside potential, more downside protection, more respect or more inspiration. Most employees--and especially consultants--won't tell you the real reason for their request unless you ask them repeatedly in different ways to describe why they're really asking for a raise.

When negotiating compensation, it's best to link employee pay with company performance rather than just link it to employee performance during the startup stage. This puts pressure on the business model to work--so everyone gets paid--and it puts pressure on team members to hold each other accountable, because their compensation is linked to each other's performance.

The downside of this incentive structure is that you may have a top-performing employee who doesn't get a salary increase or bonus because of execution problems among his or her colleagues. You should deal with this on a case-by-case basis and may want to provide occasional bonuses for exceptional performance. In practice, giving employees a gift certificate for a trip or an expensive dinner out for their family and friends may provide a better incentive than a cash bonus pool that becomes the source of tension among employees. In a small startup, a cash bonus pool to be divided among employees is a bad idea and undermines the base compensation levels you've negotiated with them.

Negotiating With Investors

Traditional negotiation theories tell you to understand your BATNA--or Best Alternative to a Negotiated Agreement--before you begin negotiations. Unfortunately, for most cash-strapped startups seeking capital from investors, your BATNA is going out business! So a negotiation theory for startups requires a different approach. Here are some tips for negotiating with investors when your BATNA is closing shop and going back to a 9-to-5 job:

1. Never let them see you sweat. Investors will only put money in a company if the entrepreneur is confident of the company's prospects. They might know you have few alternatives for startup financing, but when they see your confidence, they'll temporarily forget about those other options.

2. Draft the investment terms before the meeting. It might be putting the cart before the horse, but it's critical to have investment terms clear in your head before you meet with investors. If you're pitching venture

capital investors, get familiar with term sheets before you walk in the door.

3. Tell minority investors that you have standard terms that are non-negotiable. Don't let investors restructure your investment terms unless they plan to lead the entire round of fundraising. Most investors will actually prefer you to have standard terms so they can focus on evaluating the business proposition rather than the investment terms. Avoid the temptation to negotiate individual terms with each investor because it will likely cause you headaches down the line when certain investors are paid back before others.

Negotiating With Suppliers

During the startup stage, it's almost always a problem to negotiate favorable deals with suppliers. How can you strike a deal for a volume discount when you can't accurately forecast sales volume? How can suppliers provide you with credit when you don't have a track record with other suppliers?

I recommend negotiating with suppliers just like you'll negotiate with investors: Put your best foot forward, and let them believe in your company as much as you do. For instance, let your suppliers dream of the day when you'll be their biggest customer. Negotiating a deal on favorable terms will be considerably easier when they perceive your business as a potential long-term client rather than a startup.

One concrete way to accomplish this with a key supplier is to extend the duration of your order rather than just negotiate on price--and, to protect yourself, by adding termination provisions to the contract. Suppliers and their sales staff are more likely to provide a favorable price for a long-term agreement with a termination clause rather than to a small, low volume order. For example, if you're reasonably confident in your business's growth potential, try ordering three years' worth of supplies rather than a one-year supply. But be sure to spread out the payments over the life of the contract and add in an enforceable termination clause.

Connell Black
Business Capital Advisor

What Investors are looking for?

Can you explain your idea in 15 seconds or less?

You should be able to articulate your product/service in 15 seconds or less, leaving the audience with enough information that makes them WANT (not need) to know more.

Think with the end in mind, and work backwards
What is your end goal with your vision? Can you articulate it? How will it be operating? What will be needed in order to obtain that vision?

Think like an investor

Investors want to know:

- How much will it cost me?

- How much can I make off of this investment?

- How much have YOU invested?

- What is the risk? Is there recourse?

- How long will it take for me to make it back?

Know your numbers!

Investors, for the most part, are numbers people. They expect you to know ALL of your numbers. For example, your sales, expenses, COGS (Cost of Goods Sold), Gross/Net profits, etc. If you don't know your numbers, investors will start to tune you out as not knowing your business.

People Product Process

The 10 Most Reliable Ways to Fund a Startup

1. Seek a bank loan or credit-card line of credit.

2. Trade equity or services for startup help.

3. Negotiate an advance from a strategic partner or customer.

4. Join a startup incubator or accelerator.

5. Solicit venture-capital investors.

6. Apply to local angel-investor groups.

7. Start a crowdfunding campaign online.

8. Request a small-business grant.

9. Pitch your needs to friends and family.

10. Fund your startup yourself.

You can see that all of these options require work and

commitment on your part, so there is no magic or free money. All funding decisions have complex tradeoff between near-term and longer-term costs and paybacks, as well as overall ownership and control.

Chapter 10
Entrepreneur
Resources and Quotes

Entrepreneur Resources

Starting Your Business

After you evaluate your business idea, determine startup costs and research the market, you'll be ready to take on the next steps to starting your business.

Track your progress as you go with this business startup checklist:

Prepare a business plan that outlines your business goals, operating procedures, competitors, as well as the company's current and desired funding.

Incorporate your business or form an LLC. It provides the owner with personal asset protection from the debts and liabilities of the company.

Address necessary post-incorporation formalities.

Obtain your federal tax identification number (also called employer identification number or EIN). It's used by the IRS to identify your business for all taxation matters.

Obtain a state tax identification number. Contact your state's taxation department to determine whether your state of formation imposes this requirement.

Obtain the necessary business licenses and/or permits. Licenses may be required by your city, municipality, county and/or state. Contact your

Secretary of State and local government to ensure you meet any requirements.

Select an accountant and attorney you can turn to for advice when starting out, as well as throughout the life of the business.

Open a business bank account and obtain a business credit card. Contact your bank about business banking requirements to ensure you have all the necessary paperwork.

Set up your business accounting/bookkeeping. Be prepared to account for all disbursements, payments received, invoices, accounts receivable/payable, etc.

Establish business credit. A line of credit lessens the number of times your business must prepay for products. It also establishes a favorable credit history.

Obtain business insurance. Discuss your particular industry and business needs with your insurance agent to obtain the appropriate type and amount of insurance.

Ensure you comply with government requirements (e.g., unemployment insurance, worker's compensation, OSHA, payroll tax requirements, self-employment taxes, etc.).

Determine your business location and take these steps:

Home-based: Check zoning requirements

Other location: Lease office or retail space and obtain the necessary furniture, equipment and supplies

Create any necessary contracts, service agreements and invoices so you can easily bill customers, track payments and keep records.

Obtain business financing.

Create a logo, business cards, letterhead, envelopes, etc., to build business identity.

Secure your company's domain name with a registration website.

Create a website. A company website allows you to establish your brand and will be the first opportunity to make an impression with customers.

Create a marketing plan for your products and services. Increase the likelihood for success with a plan for promoting your products and services to your target market.

www.MyNewCompany.com

www.LegalZoom.com

www.GoDaddy.com

www.Wordpress.com

www.SBA.Gov

SCORE is a nonprofit association dedicated to helping small businesses get off the ground, grow and achieve their goals through education and mentorship. Supported by the U.S. Small Business Administration (SBA), SCORE is able to deliver services at no charge or at very low cost. For more information, visit https://www.score.org/; 1-800-634-0245.

About.com Starting a Business Hub: Another resource you should not miss is About.com's Entrepreneurs Hub. They've curated some of their best content for starting a business, including checklists, a small business startup kit, and detailed articles on naming and calculating the cost of your startup.

Library of Congress's Entrepreneur's Reference Guide: Yes, the U.S. Library of Congress has an entrepreneur's reference guide, while it's dated (1999), it also lists a lot of great books that are updated yearly. It covers practically every topic related to starting a small business.

Inspirations for the Idea

There are few things more important to the success of your startup than having the right idea and continuing to be innovative with your product as it gets built and released to your customers. Ideas don't just come in cans from the store, though.

Vator.tv: A play on "elevator pitch," Vator.tv is a place where entrepreneurs can upload short video pitches about their startup. Not only that, but you can follow industry news and specific companies. Watching these pitches will certainly jolt your brain's creative juices. Also check out VentureBeat Profiles (formerly TradeVibes), which also has a great database of startups and a community discussing each one.

Alltop Startups: Reading the latest news and opinions in the startup world can only help jolt your brain and keep you current. Alltop has a great list of blogs and news websites dedicated to the subject (including my personal blog). Take a read, subscribe to the blogs that interest you, and you'll be guaranteed to be reading about great ideas soon enough.

Startup Web Apps

While there is an array of great web tools for entrepreneurs there are some tools that just make your life easier when you're trying to bring order to the chaos of launching your startup. Consider these tools when you're in the early stages of building a company:

Evernote: Information is king, and there are few web apps that do a better job of collecting information in front of the computer screen or on-the-go than Evernote. The service simply helps you remember everything. You can take pictures of your receipts for easy organization or save key info while you browse, for example, among many other ways to organize and catalog the things you need to remember for your startup.

Zoho: Zoho is a suite of online collaboration tools. Not only does it include email and spreadsheets, but it includes, wiki, chat, customer relationship management (CRM), and web conferencing as well. While it is similar to Google Apps, it is built specifically for businesses.

PBWorks: Wikis are amazing for organizing ideas and sharing them with team members. There are few better suited for business than PBWorks, which is not only a wiki but a collaboration tool, document manager, and project management tool.

Fresh Books: If your business is client-based, you need to track invoices, teams, and payments constantly. While there are many choices, Freshbooks is one of the best due to its mobile apps, integration with Basecamp, and reasonable pricing.

Social Media for Startup Success

Social media is about connecting with people. Interestingly enough, so is business and entrepreneurship, which is perhaps why there is so much overlap between the two. If you want to get your startup off the ground, you have to network, build up your social circle, and reach out to the right people. These social tools are adept at that task:

Plaxo: Plaxo acts as a digital address book that efficiently organizes everyone you meet. Plus, it integrates with Outlook, Thunderbird and the Mac OS X Address Book to make importing contacts a snap. You have to be diligent about adding contacts, though.

GoogleWave: Google's experimental real-time communication platform not only has a consumer version, but also comes in a corporate flavor for users of Google apps. Having your team collaborate on projects through waves is a unique experience.

LinkedIn: This one may be obvious, but its importance in business cannot be overstated. It is the world's most popular business social network for a reason. Its business features, especially those connecting you to friends of friends, are unmatched, and with over 50 million users, it's a social media tool you need to be using constantly.

The Funded: This entrepreneurship community is very unique in that it is focused on helping you raise money. How? By giving you ratings and inside details of the practices of countless venture capital and angel investor funds. The information, once you're in, is invaluable to choosing the firm that will help propel your business to the next level.

How to Fund a Startup: This guide by Y Combinator co-founder and early-stage investor Paul Graham is shockingly detailed on the different ways to raise money, the disadvantages of each approach, how venture capital firms operate, and the reality of bringing investors into your company. A must-read for any startup founder before raising capital.

Startup Social Communities

You cannot and should not build your business alone. The world's greatest entrepreneurs not only had co-founders, but they had friends, family, and a community of entrepreneurs and advisors that helped them with difficult decisions, overcoming adversity, and fixing mistakes.

With the rise of social media and the web, incredible startup communities have popped up, each one with a unique character but with a wealth of community knowledge that you'd be crazy to pass up on your journey to build a great company.

Startup Nation: The recently redesigned startup community network has extensive and active forums, useful knowledge hubs, community groups, and plenty more.

Hacker News: The seed investment firm Y Combinator has built a thriving and active startup community known as Hacker News. Users add relevant and interesting stories on the topics of programming and startup entrepreneurship and consistently hold thought-provoking discussions. It's an incredible place for insight and advice on startups.

YoungEntrepreneur: Focused around discussion forums, Young Entrepreneur is a great place to ask any startup question on your mind or just to read the over 240,000 posts made over the years on the site.

PartnerUp: PartnerUp is a community that really focuses on one thing: helping you find business partners. In business, finding the right co-founders is often the difference between stellar success and a quick, painful startup death. PartnerUp is a community ideal for finding and networking with people that will shore up your weaknesses and help you answer those nagging questions about the partnership side of business.

StartUpTN: Startup Tennessee is leading entrepreneurship across the state, as part of Governor Haslam's initiative to create high growth businesses in Tennessee. THREE out of FIVE new jobs come from companies that are less than five years old — "startups"! www.startuptn.com

Google for Entrepreneurs: Since 2011, we've launched Campuses and formed partnerships that support entrepreneurs across 125 countries.

www.googleforentrepreneurs.com

Nashville Entrepreneur Center: www.ec.co

www.Grants.Gov

www.YolandaSpeaks.Biz

Best Entrepreneurial Tools, Guides, and Resources:

BusinessFinance.com: the site for entrepreneurs to find thousands of sources for business loans, venture capital, equipment leasing, and commercial real estate financing — as well as the guidance and tips for helping you obtain the financing you need for your business.

Business Town: a small business resource portal, with information for starting and managing a small business, preparing a business plan, and obtaining guidance for accounting, advertising, hiring, legal issues, managing employees, marketing, and sales.

CrowdSPRING: a creative resource for entrepreneurs and small businesses looking for creative and branding services, including logo development, Website design, and copywriting assistance. Post your project, along with a price you're willing to pay, and work with dozens of creatives and pick your favorite from an average of 110+ custom concepts.

Entrepreneur.com: simply an amazing collection of resources for current and prospective entrepreneurs, and a great place to find all sorts of tools and guides for starting your own business.

Forbes.com: Entrepreneurs and Small Business News and Information — get advice and information on starting and growing a small business from the editors at Forbes.com.

goBIGnetwork: a good networking site for entrepreneurs, designed to help connect startups, investors, job seekers, advisors and service providers..

Inc.com: the website for Inc. magazine, delivering advice, tools, and services, to help business owners and CEOs start, run, and grow their businesses more successfully.

morebusiness.com: a site by entrepreneurs for entrepreneurs, and designed to be a comprehensive resource for small businesses. It contains tips, articles, ideas, templates, worksheets, sample business plans, tools, financial benchmarks, sample contracts, and much more to help grow your business.

U.S. Small Business Administration: an independent agency of the federal government whose purpose is to aid, counsel, assist, and protect the interests of small business concerns. The site includes information and resources for planning, starting, growing, and ending your business. Some great tools here.

Startup Journal: The Wall Street Journal Center for Entrepreneurs — offering solutions to problems facing small companies. Lots of different topics, including profiles of firms dealing with each topic. Also includes a discussion board where you can exchange ideas with small-business owners and other readers.

ZeroMillion.com — an entrepreneurial resources and networking site founded by the author of Zero to One Million, a step-by-step guide to starting your own business and building it to one million dollars in sales. The mission of the site is to encourage and support entrepreneurial endeavors internationally.

Social Media Tools for Small Business

Dashboards / Management Tools

SocialBro

TweetDeck

Tweetcaster

Twitter Tools

Followerwonk

Social Rank

ManageFlitter

Must Be Present

Tweriod

Tweepi

Tweet4Me

Commun.it

Twtrland

NeedTagger

TweeterSpy

Twitter Feed

TweetReach

Twazzup

Topsy

Facebook Tools

LikeAlyzer

Wolfram Alpha Facebook Report

Facebook Custom Audiences

Social Media Analytics Tools

Rival IQ

Buzz Sumo

Klout

SharedCount

Google URL Builder

Visual Content Tools

Infogr.am

Piktochart

Visually

Canva

Compfight

LICEcap

Social Media Monitoring Tools

Nutshell

MailSocial

Mention

Keyhole

Social Media Content Tools

News.me

Feedly

Pocket

Paper.li

Swayy

Pie

Bottlenose

WordPress Plugins

Digg Digg

Flare

Ivy

Pin It Button for Images

Miscellaneous Tools

Fivehundredplus

Rapportive

Bitly

Rev

Pinterest Board Cover Creator

Jelly

Google+ Page Audit

Powtoon

Cardmunch

IFTTT

Zapier

Buffer

Talking to Customers

Intercom: tasteful chat and help widgets for your site, plus good automated email triggers
Drip--email courses and signup widgets for your site

Mailchimp: newsletters and decent signup widgets

Buffer: easier way to run your twitter and Facebook accounts

Team collaboration

Slack: chat and messaging to reduce internal email load, with one room per major project

Github: repository for your source code plus task lists and collaboration with your developers

Dropbox: all company files should be here, not on email attachments or personal folders

Streak: simple CRM plugin for Gmail to manage and share your sales leads

Trello: digital kanban board for project management

Basecamp: I use it for project management with external teams who don't know our Trello workflow

Stormboard: digital sticky notes for remote brainstorming and workshops

Meldium: team password sharing and management
Domains

Lean Domain Search: suggests all available .coms with a given keyword somewhere in the name

Instant Domain Search: quickly check specific domain availability

Namecheap: register your domains without getting screwed Payments

Square (US) or iZettle: accept credit card payments with your phone, e.g. for market stalls and contractors

Stripe: best payment processing online

GoCardless: (UK)--accept direct debit payments

Gumroad: easily sell digital files like PDFs, videos, and links

Analytics

Google Analytics: free and good enough for all your analytics needs

Google Keyword Planner--see how many people are searching relevant terms

Facebook Ads--use the targeting options to compare the approximate size and location of various interests and demographics

Physical Products and Print-on-Demand

Createspace: upload a PDF, sell a printed book via Amazon

Newspaper Club: ever wanted your own newspaper?
The Game Crafter--prototype and sell your board and card games

Shapeways: high quality 3d printing in a wide range of materials including gold and silver (for jewelry) and ceramics (for household goods); great for prototyping and market-testing physical products

Alibaba: cut out the middle man and buy anything you want directly from the manufacturer; if you've ever wanted a 40' shipping container full of go karts, this is the place for you

Building Websites

Squarespace: visual site builder with good themes and integrations with stores, payments, newsletters, etc

Strikingly: easy site builder for nice single-page sites like manifestos, personal/company pages, or landing pages

Shopify: for ecommerce and online stores

Themeforest: if you need something custom, start by buying a $30 theme and editing it

Art

Glyphicons: icon set
500px--non-cheesy stock photography

Flickr Creative commons: search for photos with the appropriate usage rights

Subtle Patterns: pretty much what it says on the tin; for backgrounds and textures

Fiverr: pay $5 (or a bit more) for tasks ranging from logo design to copywriting

99designs: crowdsource design tasks (especially logos) for a few hundred dollars

Elance: various freelancers (assume you'll hire several for trial projects before finding good ones)

Clarity.fm: pay-by-the-minute advice from various startup specialists

Dribbble: browse designer portfolios, many of whom also freelance

TextIt: create SMS applications without programming (e.g. for the developing world)

Twilio: makes phone calls and SMS as easy to program as websites

Legals

Docracy: open source legal documents

Companies Made Simple (UK): set up and manage a UK corporation for 19

Duedil (UK): nice interface over companies house interface to research industry and competitors

Learning

Paul Graham's Essays--read the whole archive

Tropical MBA: 250 podcast episodes comprising the best source of knowledge on location independence and manufacturing businesses

News

Hacker News--daily news for startup folks and hackers

Product Hunt--daily new products
Investors

f6s--listing of all accelerator programs (and lots of other info) and a social network for startups and angels

AngelList: social network and funding platform for startups and angels

Capitallist: like Angellist, but focused on London and the UK

The Funded: reviews and testimonials of investors from the founders' perspective; do your investor due diligence here

Crowdfunding

Crowdcube (UK)--equity crowd funding

Seedrs (UK): equity crowd funding

Kickstarter: crowd-fund via pre-selling your products

Indiegogo: crowd-fund via donations with a focus on arts and creative projects, including some

Great Book for Entrepreneurs

Rework by Jason Fried & David Heinemeier Hansson

Purple Cow by Seth Godin

The 7 Habits of Highly Effective People by Stephen Covey

Choose Yourself by James Altucher

The only skills you need to be an entrepreneur are the ability to fail, to have ideas, to sell those ideas, to execute on them, and to be persistent so even as you fail you learn and move onto the next adventure. James Altucher

Tribes by Seth Godin

Creative Confidence by Tom and David Kelly

How to Win Friends and Influence People by Dale Carnegie

The Psychology of Selling by Brian Tracy

Rich Dad, Poor Dad by Robert Kiyosaki and Sharon Lechter

Rich Woman by Kim Kiyosaki

Thinking, Fast and Slow by Daniel Kahneman

The E-Myth Revisited by Michael E. Gerber

Founders at Work by Jessica Livingston

"The Power of Habit" by Charles Duhigg

See You at the Top by Zig Ziglar

The 21 Irrefutable Laws of Leadership by John C. Maxwell

EntreLeadership: 20 Years of Practical Business Wisdom from the Trenches

by Dave Ramsey

Jesus CEO: Using Ancient Wisdom for Visionary Leadership by Laurie Beth Jones

The Startup Playbook: Secrets of the Fastest-Growing Startups From Their Founding Entrepreneurs by David Kidder

Creativity Inc: Overcoming the Unseen Forces That Stand in the Way of True Inspiration by Ed Catmull

True North by Bill George and Peter Sims

Zero to One: Notes Startups, or How to Build the Future by Peter Thiel

Abundance: The Future is Better Than You Think by Peter Diamandis and Steven Kotler

The 4-Hour Workweek by Timothy Ferriss

The Fire Starter Sessions by Danielle LaPorte

The $100 Startup by Chris Guillebeau

Enchantment by Guy Kawasaki

A Curious Mind: The Secret to a Bigger Life, by Brian Grazer

The Road to Character by David Brooks

The Wright Brothers by David McCullough

Entrepreneur Quotes

"My biggest motivation? Just to keep challenging myself. I see life almost like one long University education that I never had — everyday I'm learning something new."

–Richard Branson, founder Virgin Group

"Every time you state what you want or believe, you're the first to hear it. It's a message to both you and others about what you think is possible. Don't put a ceiling on yourself."

– Oprah Winfrey, media proprietor

"Your work is going to fill a large part of your life, and the only way to be truly satisfied is to do what you believe is great work. And the only way to do great work is to love what you do."

– Steve Jobs, Co-founder, CEO, Chairman Apple Inc.

"I knew that if I failed I wouldn't regret that, but I knew the one thing I might regret is not trying."

–Jeff Bezos, founder and CEO Amazon

"Whether you think you can, or think you can't — you're right."

– Henry Ford, Founder Ford Motor Company

"Don't limit yourself. Many people limit themselves to what they think they can do. You can go as

"You don't learn to walk by following rules. You learn by doing and falling over."

– Richard Branson, founder Virgin Group

"When you find an idea that you just can't stop thinking about, that's probably a good one to pursue."

–Josh James, co-founder and CEO Omniture, founder and CEO Domo

"It's not about ideas. It's about making ideas happen."

– Scott Belsky, co-founder Behance2

"Entrepreneur is someone who has a vision for something and a want to create."

– David Karp, founder and CEO Tumblr

"The only thing worse than starting something and failing… is not starting something."

– Seth Godin, founder Squidoo

"When I'm old and dying, I plan to look back on my life and say 'wow, that was an adventure,' not 'wow, I sure felt safe.' "Tom Preston-Werner, Github co-founder

– Tom Preston-Werner, co-founder Github

"The fastest way to change yourself is to hang out with people who are already the way you want to be."

– Reid Hoffman, co-founder Li2nkedIn

"I don't look to jump over 7-foot bars — I look for 1-foot bars that I can step over."

"In the end, a vision without the ability to execute it is probably a hallucination."

– Steve Case, co-founder AOL

"Fearlessness is like a muscle. I know from my own life that the more I exercise it the more natural it becomes to not let my fears run me."

– Arianna Huffington, president and editor in chief The Huffington Post Media Group

"Embrace what you don't know, especially in the beginning, because what you don't know can become your greatest asset. It ensures that you will absolutely be doing things different from everybody else."

– Sara Blakely, founder SPANX

"Risk more than others think is safe. Dream more than others think is practical."

–Howard Schultz, Starbucks CEO

"The way to get started is to quit talking and begin doing."

– Walt Disney, founder Disney

"High expectations are the key to everything."

– Sam Walton, founder Walmart

"Don't be afraid to assert yourself, have confidence in your abilities and don't let the bastards get you down."

– Michael Bloomberg, founder Bloomberg L.P.

"There's lots of bad reasons to start a company. But there's only one good, legitimate reason, and I think you know what it is: it's to change the world."

– Phil Libin, CEO Evernote

"The important thing is not being afraid to take a chance. Remember, the greatest failure is to not try. Once you find something you love to do, be the best at doing it."

– Debbi Fields, found Mrs. Fields Cookies

"You shouldn't focus on why you can't do something, which is what most people do. You should focus on why perhaps you can, and be one of the exceptions."

– Steve Case, co-founder AOL

"Empower yourself and realize the importance of contributing to the world by living your talent. Work on what you love. You are responsible for the talent that has been entrusted to you."

– Catharina Bruns, Founder Work Is Not a Job

"You shouldn't focus on why you can't do something, which is what most people do. You should focus on why perhaps you can, and be one of the exceptions."

– Steve Case, co-founder AOL

Building a company from the ground up and successfully running it is hard-work. Without the right work ethics your business will never thrive and grow.

"The price of success is hard work, dedication to the job at hand, and the determination that whether we win or lose, we have applied the best of ourselves to the task at hand."– Vince Lombardi, executive, head coach, player NFL

"I'm convinced that about half of what separates the successful entrepreneurs from the non-successful ones is pure perseverance."– Steve Jobs, Co-founder, CEO, Chairman Apple Inc.

"I've missed more than 9,000 shots in my career. I've lost almost 300 games. 26 times I've been trusted to take the game winning shot and missed. I've failed over and over and over again in my life and that is why I succeed."

–Michael Jordan, NBA Legendary Basketball MVP

"Chase the vision, not the money; the money will end up following you." –Tony Hsieh, Zappos CEO

"The critical ingredient is getting off your butt and doing something. It's as simple as that. A lot of people have ideas, but there are few who decide to do something about them now. Not tomorrow. Not next week. But today. The true entrepreneur is a doer, not a dreamer." – Nolan Bushnell, Entrepreneur

"Your work is going to fill a large part of your life, and the only way to be truly satisfied is to do what you believe is great work. And the only way to do great work is to love what you do." –Steve Jobs, Co-Founder, Chairman and CEO, Apple

"I'm convinced that about half of what separates the successful entrepreneurs from the non-successful ones is pure perseverance." –Steve Jobs, Co-Founder of Apple

"Choose a job that you like, and you will never have to work a day in your life." -Confucius, Philosopher

chalk drawing of Einstein and formula3. "A person who never made a mistake never tried anything new." -Albert Einstein, Physicist

"Stay self-funded as long as possible." -Garrett Camp, Co-Founder of Uber

"If you are going through hell, keep going." -Winston Churchill, British Prime Minister

"The greater danger for most of us lies not in setting our aim too high and falling short, but in setting our aim too low and achieving our mark." -Michelangelo, Artist

"Business opportunities are like buses: there's always another one coming." –Richard Branson

EPILOGUE

Entrepreneurship Is Mindset not a Storefront book offers a refreshingly practical blueprint for thinking and acting in entrepreneur environments that are fast-paced, rapidly changing, and highly uncertain. It provides both a guide to equipping those that have chosen to launch out and start their own business. It helps you to find tomorrow's opportunities and a set of entrepreneurial principles you can use personally to transform the arenas in which you compete. I hope I have presented simple but powerful ways to help you stop thinking and acting by the old rules and start thinking with the discipline of a habitual entrepreneur.

You can do this by eliminating paralyzing uncertainty by creating an entrepreneurial mindset that shapes a shared understanding of what is to be accomplished; create a richly stocked opportunity register to redesign existing products, find new sources of innovative ideas in existing markets, reconfigure market spaces, and seize the huge breakthroughs; build a dynamic portfolio of businesses and options that continuously move your organization toward the future; execute dynamic ideas so that you can move fast, with confidence and without undue risk; and develop your own way of leading with an entrepreneurial mindset to create a sustainable entrepreneurial climate within your organization.

Starting a new business is not an easy task; however, despite the obstacles, many entrepreneurs work hard in order to achieve success. Many successful entrepreneurs are extremely passionate about their business ideas. This passion is what motivates them to go above and beyond an ordinary individual. They tend to remain strong even through the toughest of times and learn from mistakes. In addition, they are also organized individuals who are well-prepared to present their funding proposal, elevator pitch, and business plans to prospective investors.

Many successful entrepreneurs are also enthusiastic risk takers who are not afraid of failure. Last, they are able to find a balance between family and work life and have the unconditional support of their family. Having the right mindset will help each entrepreneur not only start the business but sustain it.

To be successful in sustainable business practices often requires entrepreneurship mindset and innovation. The importance of entrepreneurship mindset and innovation also applies to companies that change how they produce products and services.

MAIN TAKEAWAYS

To be successful in sustaining your business it requires entrepreneurship mindset and innovation.

- Entrepreneurship Mindset and innovation are relevant in for-profit and nonprofit ventures.

- Entrepreneurship Mindset can be viewed as recognizing change, pursuing opportunity, taking on risk and responsibility, innovating, making better use of resources, creating new value that is meaningful to customers, and doing it all over again and again.

- Being an entrepreneur requires taking on significant responsibility and comes with significant challenges and potential rewards.

- Entrepreneurship is a mind-set, an attitude; it is taking a particular approach to doing things.

- The motivations for becoming an entrepreneur are diverse and can include the potential for financial reward, the pursuit of personal values and interests, and the interest in social change.

- Entrepreneurship is more than about opening an office or storefront

- Successful entrepreneurship often requires creativity and innovation in addressing a new opportunity or concern in a new way.

Dedication

Robert Brooks
December 4, 1918-1983

I dedicate this book "Entrepreneurship is a Mindset not a Storefront" to my Grandfather Robert Brooks, business owner and my role model. His impressive career advancement despite only having a junior high school education inspired me to believe that I was capable of doing anything I put my mind to. He was born in Oklahoma City, lived in California for a short period and then moved to Anchorage Alaska to work in the construction industry. After several years as a construction worker and master carpenter he started his own business in construction and property management and rental. He also opened Brooks Tool and Auto Rental.

He had one of the first car and tool rental businesses in Anchorage Alaska. Because of him I am who I am today.

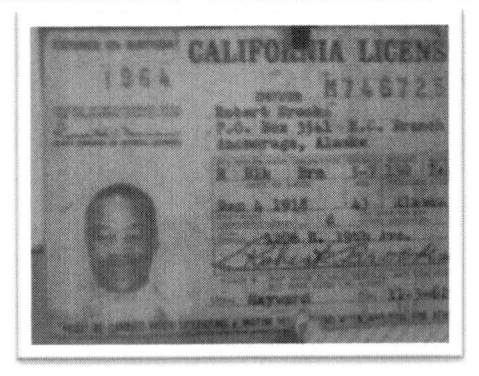

"Don't limit yourself. Many people limit themselves to what they think they can do. You can go as far as your mind lets you. What you believe, remember, you can achieve." – Mary Kay Ash, Founder Mary Kay Cosmetics

NOTES

ENTREPRENUERSHIP A MINDSET NOT A STOREFRONT

Yolanda Conley Shields

ENTREPRENUERSHIP A MINDSET NOT A STOREFRONT

Yolanda Conley Shields

ENTREPRENUERSHIP A MINDSET NOT A STOREFRONT

Yolanda Conley Shields

ENTREPRENUERSHIP A MINDSET NOT A STOREFRONT

BUSINESS GOAL

MARKETING GOALS

NETWORKING CONTACTS

VISION STATEMENT

PITCH NOTES

ABOUT THE AUTHOR

Yolanda Conley Shields , Author, Speaker, Coach and CEO understands that she was born to be an entrepreneur and a change agent. She sees her work as a calling and not just a job. She is a much sought after speaker and trainer in the area of business development, nonprofit management and social entrepreneurship and has traveled extensively throughout the United States, France and Africa. She also does community development work in the continent of Africa and other 3rd World Countries. She has earned degrees in the field of Education and Social Work MBA2016. She has several certifications in the area of grant writing, small business development, education, nonprofit management and fund development. She has been appointed by Tennessee Governor Bill Haslam to the Labor and Workforce Development Board for the State of Tennessee and Co-Chairs the Oversight Committee. For many years she has devoted her life to helping others, so it's no surprise that she is seen as a gifted leader and advocate. She has assisted over 20 corporations (For-profit and Non-Profit) in the areas of strategic planning, business operations, international community development, workforce development, fund development, celebrity charity management, HRM, and organizational sustainability. www.YolandaSpeaks.Biz

She has worked with such celebrities as CeCe Winans, Darrell Green, Art Monk, Tony Boselli, and many others. She desires to serve with integrity and leaves nothing less than a trail of excellence wherever she's involved. Yolanda released her first book Letters to Our Sons in 2013 www.Lettertooursons.com and looking forward to the impact her new book "Entrepreneurship is a Mindset not a Storefront" will have on many business owner and leaders.

You can follow Yolanda on all of her social *media sites at*
Twitter ~ YESBuilds
Facebook ~ YESBuilds
Facebook ~ Letterstooursons
Twitter ~ Lettertooursons
Instagram ~ YESBuilds
YouTube ~ Yolanda Conley Shields
www.YolandaSpeaks.Biz
www.YESBuilds.com

Letters to Our Sons Book and Journal

Book and Journal Available on Amazon.com

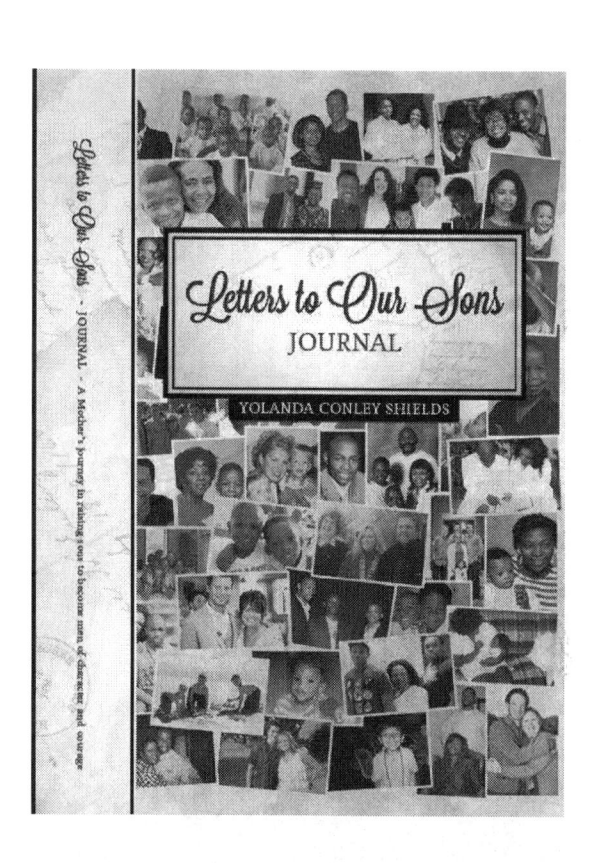

Book and Journal Available on Amazon.com

Made in the USA
Charleston, SC
03 May 2016